Trees

of the

Great
Lakes
Reaion

D0851337

By Joseph S. Illick
Steve Harrington

Trees of the Great Lakes Region

was originally published as ***Common Trees of Michigan*** by the American Tree Association. This edition is a reprint of that work and has been significantly updated and edited.

Printed in the USA
ISBN: 0-9624629-2-6

Cover Photo: Stand of hardwoods reflected in the Grand River, Kent County, Michigan by Steve Harrington.

One cannot pluck a flower without troubling a star.
--Francis Thompson

Contents

Trees

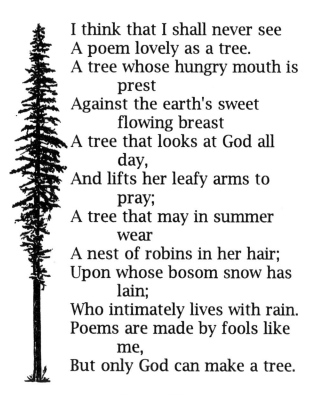

I think that I shall never see
A poem lovely as a tree.
A tree whose hungry mouth is
    prest
Against the earth's sweet
    flowing breast
A tree that looks at God all
    day,
And lifts her leafy arms to
    pray;
A tree that may in summer
    wear
A nest of robins in her hair;
Upon whose bosom snow has
    lain;
Who intimately lives with rain.
Poems are made by fools like
    me,
But only God can make a tree.

--Joyce Kilmer

Introduction

One does not need to know the names of trees to appreciate them. It is enough to enjoy the shade and beauty they provide.

One does not need to know if leaves are simple or compound. It is enough to hear them rustle in a solemn autumn breeze.

One does not need to know about the flowers and fruits of trees. It is enough to inhale the dense, sweet aroma of black locust blossoms on an early summer evening.

One does not need to know many things about trees to appreciate them. This is true. But knowing their names is fun and helps them become familiar in our minds. Eventually, they become old friends and a walk in the woodlot is a reunion of fond memories.

It is not my intention to dwell on the scientific aspects of trees. I am certain, for example, that a white oak cares not if you call it *Quercus alba* or Rover. But if you are ready to learn about trees and enjoy them as old friends along a wooded trail, then the information found on these pages will serve you well.

These pages will help you learn the fascinating and sometimes remarkable stories each species has to tell. You may learn that the black locust trees that scent your early summer evenings are considered "weeds" by some but early shipbuilders found their hard wood ideal for wooden nails, with which they could secure deck planks to sleek schooners. Or that French monarch King Louis IV so loved the flowers and fragrance that he had black locusts planted in his royal gardens, thus introducing the tree to Europe.

Or perhaps you will learn that the sugar and red maples provide a bounty of sweet sap each spring. You may be surprised to learn American Indians found ways to evaporate the sap and turn the nectar into sugar to flavor game.

These pages will serve you well, if you wish. Be open to discoveries and the exploration of the natural world around you.

---Steve Harrington
July 1998

White Pine
Pinus strobus

There is no tree in the world that surpasses the white pine in beauty, stateliness, individuality, and usefulness. It is the prince of North American trees. Reliable records show that the first American house was built of white pine.

It is the only evergreen tree native to eastern North America that has soft, slender, flexible, straight, bluish-green leaves grouped in clusters of five. They are 3 to 5 inches long and persist for 2 years.

The cones are 5 to 10 inches long, short-stalked, narrowly cylindrical, and rarely hang long on the trees. The cone scales are thin, flat, and without spines or prickles. The trunk is straight, when grown in dense stands it is clear of branches for many feet. The lateral branches occur in whorls of 3 to 7 arranged in horizontal layers. Upon falling they leave distinct circles of branch scars. The wood is soft, light brown, straight-grained, and easily worked. It is used for a wider range of purposes than any American wood.

The white pine has been planted for reforestation and ornamentation. Originally it formed pure stands over vast areas of the Great Lakes region. It was an important natural resource during the lumbering era of the late 1800s.

White Pine

Range: The white pine is native only to eastern North America. It is found from Newfoundland west to Manitoba and Minnesota southward to Pennsylvania and Illinois and along the mountains to Georgia. It occurs throughout the Great Lakes region.

Red Pine

Pinus resinosa

The red pine, also called Norway pine, is one of the most important pine trees native to North America.

The leaves are straight, slender, flexible, 4 to 6 inches long and occur in pairs. They are usually tufted at the end of the branches and persist for 3 to 5 years. They break cleanly when doubled.

The cones are egg-shaped, about 2 inches long, usually without stalks. It has no prickles on the cone scales.

The bark is thick, reddish-brown, marked with shallow furrows, and peels off into thin scales. The twigs are stout and orange brown.

The wood is rather hard, pale red, with thin light sapwood. It is used for nearly all the purposes for which white pine is used.

The red pine rarely exceeds 70 to 80 feet in height and 3 feet in diameter. It has few enemies, grows rapidly, and if given care and protection, will produce large quantities of high quality wood.

The red pine has been planted extensively for reforestation and ornamentation purposes. Large tracts of state and national forests are planted with rows of red pines. Originally the red pine occurred in pure stands or in a mixture with white pines.

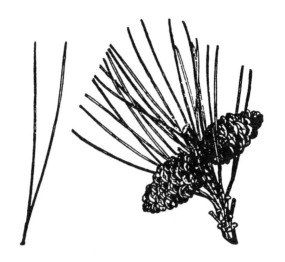

Red Pine

Range: The red pine is found from Nova Scotia south to central Pennsylvania and west to Michigan and Minnesota. In Michigan, red pine occurs chiefly in dry woods and sandy plains. It is abundant northward from the central portion of the states of Minnesota, Wisconsin, and Michigan.

Jack Pine

Pinus banksiana

The jack pine, also called gray pine and scrub pine, is a slender-trunked tree of the north woods. It covers vast areas of barren lands and extensive sand dunes. The leaves are needle-shaped, ¾ to 1¼ inches long, rather stout, generally curved and twisted, and occur in clusters of two.

The fruit is an oblong, conical, strongly curved cone 1½ to 2 inches long, without stalks, usually stands erect, and may persist for many years. The cone scales are thick at the apex and armed with very small prickles, which usually fall off early. The twigs are slender, at first pale yellowish-green, later becoming dark purplish brown. On the main stem, the bark is dark brown, slightly tinged with red, and peels off into narrow scales.

The wood is light, soft, weak, pale brown to orange. The sapwood is thick and whitish. It is used for pulpwood and manufactured into ties, slack cooperage, and lumber.

The jack pine rarely exceeds 50 feet and 18 inches in diameter. It is usually found on dry, sandy soil. In many areas it covers vast areas of barren land. It is a heavy natural reseeder after fire and it is much used as a "filler" in red pine plantings. It is well adapted to reclaiming sandy soils and serving as a nurse tree for other species.

Jack Pine

Range: The jack pine is found from Nova Scotia westward to British Columbia and south through New England to New York, northern Illinois, Michigan, and central Minnesota. It is a common tree where receding glaciers have left sandy soils behind in the northern Great Lakes region.

Scotch Pine

Pinus sylvestris

The Scotch pine, a native of and widely
distributed in western Europe, has been widely
planted in the U.S. It has been planted rather widely
for ornamental purposes and many trees were once
planted for reforestation.

A considerable number of poor stands of Scotch
pine have developed from small trees planted in the
past. It is quite probable that the main reason for
this is a poor seed supply for it develops a good
form and produces good wood in many places in its
native home in Europe.

The Scotch pine can be distinguished from other
Michigan pines by its reddish bark on the upper
third of the mature stems, and its bluish-green
needles which occur in 2's and are 2½ to 3½ inches
long.

Its conical, often lopsided 1½ to 2½-inch long
cones, which usually point backward, are also
distinctive. This tree is easy to plant, grows rapidly,
yields good wood, and is often used as a Christmas
tree.

In Europe, this tree is an important source of
timber. In the Great Lakes region it is well-suited to
sandy soils where it is sometimes planted in
extensive plantations.

Scotch Pine

Range: The Scotch pine is found throughout much of the Great Lakes region in areas where it has been planted as an ornamental, for reforestation, or in Christmas tree plantations. It prefers sandy soils and does not grow well in the rocky to clay soils of the northern portion of the Great Lakes region.

Austrian Pine
Pinus laricio

The Austrian pine, also called black pine, is a native to the mountainous regions of eastern Europe. It was one of the first evergreen trees introduced into America.

For many years it was extensively planted in parks and estates as a specimen tree. It is not native to the Great Lakes region but has been planted locally as an ornamental tree. It can often been seen in yards, parks, playgrounds, and other landscaped areas.

One who is familiar with the native red pine will see a close similarity between it and the Austrian pine. The needles of both occur in pairs and are almost identical in shape and size, but those of the Austrian pine are stiff and sharp-pointed, while those of the red pine are slender and flexible, and not so sharp-pointed.

The cones of the Austrian pine are somewhat larger than those of the red pine, and the cone scales of the former usually bear small spines; those of the latter are without spines. Other characteristics by which the Austrian pine can be recognized are its yellowish-brown winter twigs, its whitish buds, and its dark grayish-brown bark. This tree is noted for its rapidity of growth and is rather free from attacks of insects and diseases.

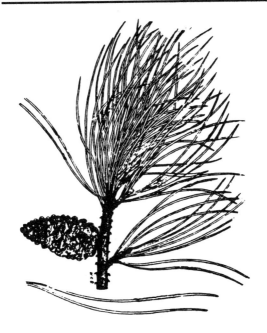

Austrian Pine

Range: The Austrian pine is a European species grown in the Great Lakes region as an ornamental. As a result it is found throughout the region in connection with landscaping around homes and parks.

Tamarack

Larix laricina

The tamarack, also called American larch, is a northern tree. It stands out prominently among its associates because it sheds all its leaves in autumn.

The leaves are flat, soft, slender and about one inch long. On the twigs of last season's growth, they occur singly; on the spurs of older twigs they are found in clusters of ten or more.

The cones are among the smallest of any American tree. They average 2/5 of an inch in length, bear about 12 scales, and often persist for many years.

The glossy brown twigs are without foliage in winter and covered with numerous stubby spurs. The bark on older trunks is reddish-brown and breaks up into small roundish scales.

The wood is heavy, hard, and durable in contact with the soil. It is used for posts, poles, ties, and in shipbuilding.

The tamarack rarely exceeds 50 feet in height and 2 feet in diameter, but sometimes reaches a height of 80 or more feet.

The European larch *(Larix decidua)* has been planted locally in the region. The European cousin has larger and usually erect cones, stouter and yellower twigs and longer and more abundant leaves. It is used extensively for reforestation.

Tamarack

Range: The tamarack is found from Newfoundland south to northern New Jersey and Pennsylvania and west to Minnesota and through British Columbia to Alaska. In the Great Lakes region, this tree occurs in cold, deep swamps. In the northern portions of the region it is also found on drier uplands.

Hemlock

Tsuga canadensis

The hemlock is an important forest tree with a very pleasing and graceful appearance. As an ornamental tree, it has few equals and as a timber tree, it stands in the front rank.

The leaves are flat, ½ inch long, rounded or notched at the apex, dark green and glossy above with two white lines on the lower surface. They are joined to the twigs by short and slender woody stalks. The leaves are spirally arranged, but appear as if arranged in two flat rows alongside the twigs. A third row of small leaves point forward on the top of the twigs.

The cones are oblong, light brown, ¾ of an inch long, and short-stalked. They often persist through the winter. The cone scales are about as wide as long.

The outer bark is reddish-brown and scaly; the inner bark is cinnamon red. The twigs are very slender, grayish-grown, at first hairy, and rough when needle-leaves are shed.

The wood is hard, weak, brittle, liable to splinter and difficult to work. It is used for coarse lumber, boxes, crates, and pulp.

The hemlock prefers moist and fertile soils. It is a shade-loving tree and usually reaches a height of 60 to 80 feet.

Hemlock

Range: The hemlock is found from Nova Scotia to
Minnesota and south to New Jersey and
Pennsylvania and along the mountains to Alabama.
It is found generally throughout the Great Lakes
region although it is relatively rare in eastern
Michigan.

Balsam Fir

Abies balsamea

The balsam fir, also called balsam, fir, and blister pine, is the favorite Christmas tree of the Americans and one of our most beautiful evergreen trees. Most people who have visited the homelands of this tree have a lasting impression of its rare beauty.

The leaves are flat, stalkless, blunt-pointed, ¾ of an inch long, deep green on the upper surface, and pale green with two white lines on the lower surface. They are spirally arranged, but appear to be in two flat rows.

The cones are 2 to 4 inches long, cylindrical in outline, and stand erect on twigs. The cone scales fall off shortly after maturing and leave only a bare cone axis.

The bark is smooth, grayish-brown, and dotted with projecting balsam blisters. Upon puncturing them, a clear balsam flows. The twigs are rather stout, grayish-brown, and smooth. The buds are egg-shaped, blunt-pointed, glossy, and about ⅛ of an inch long, clustered at the ends of twigs.

The wood is soft, pale brown, not strong nor durable. It is used chiefly for crates, boxes, and pulp. It is widely planted throughout the region in plantations for use as Christmas trees and as an ornamental.

Balsam Fir

Range: The balsam fir is a tree of the north woods. It is found from Labrador to Manitoba and Minnesota and south to Pennsylvania and along the mountains to Virginia. It is found throughout most of the Great Lakes region, especially in the northern portions.

White Spruce

Picea glauca

The white spruce, also called cat spruce, is a vigorous and handsome tree of the north woods. It is distributed widely, has a broad, pyramidal crown, and reaches a height of 50 to 60 feet and a diameter of 1 to 2 feet.

The leaves are awl-shaped, 4-sided, bluish-green needles about ¾ of an inch long. They persist for several years and are ill-scented when bruised.

The fruit is a slender, oblong, cylindrical, stalkless cone from 1 to 2 inches long.

The bark on old trunks is thin and light grayish-brown. It separates in thin scales. The twigs are grayish-green to orange-brown. The buds are light brown, broadly ovate, blunt-pointed, about ⅛ to ¼ of an inch long.

The wood is soft, weak, straight-grained and light yellow. It weighs about 32 pounds per cubic foot when dry and is used chiefly for pulp.

The white spruce prefers damp woods, banks of streams, and borders of lakes but it can also occur on relatively dry upland soils.

It grows best where winters are cold and is used significantly as an ornamental tree and as Christmas trees. It has an attractive form and often grows rapidly in northern portions of the Great Lakes region.

White Spruce

Range: The white spruce is a trans-continental tree. It is found from Labrador and Newfoundland to Alaska and south through New England to New York, Michigan, Minnesota, and northern Montana. It is generally distributed throughout the northern portions of the Great Lakes region.

Black Spruce
Picea mariana

The black spruce, also called swamp spruce and
spruce pine, is a small to medium-size tree rarely
exceeding 50 feet in height and 18 inches in
diameter.

The leaves are about ½ of an inch long, 4-sided,
blunt-pointed, and dark bluish-green.

The cones are about 1 inch long, ovoid, and
short-stalked. They mature in one year and often
persist for years. They droop from the twigs and are
sometimes used for Christmas crafts such as wreath
making.

The bark is thin, gray-brown and separates into
thin scales. The twigs become dull reddish-brown
and rusty hairy.

The wood is light, soft, white to pale yellowish.
It is used extensively for pulp and occasionally for
lumber.

This tree is believed to be closely related to the
red spruce and an increasing number of authorities
are combining the two as black spruce. This tree is
usually closely associated with the balsam fir and
the tamarack.

The black spruce prefers a moist environment so
it is commonly found in or near bogs, swamps,
banks of streams, and along lake shores.

Black Spruce

Range: The black spruce is a trans-continental tree as it extends from Labrador to Alaska and southward to northern New Jersey, Pennsylvania, Michigan, and Wisconsin. It is more common in the northern portions of the Great Lakes region.

Norway Spruce
Picea abies

The Norway spruce is not native of the region but it has been planted so extensively for ornamental purposes that it may be regarded as a naturalized tree.

The leaves are ½ to 1 inch long, 4-sided, dark green, sharp-pointed, and attached to twigs by short and slender stalk-like projections of bark.

The cones are 4 to 7 inches long, cylindrical without stalks or very short-stalked. They usually hang down from the ends of branches. The cone scales are thin, broad, reddish-brown, and finely toothed along the margin. No other spruce tree in the region has such large cones.

The bark on old trunks is roughened by rather large reddish-brown scales. The twigs are light reddish-brown, roughened by projecting leaf bases. On older trees they often assume a characteristic drooping or weeping habit.

The wood is light, soft, white, straight-grained, and easily worked. Heartwood and sapwood are not distinguishable from each other. The wood is used for paper pulp, interior finishing, and baskets.

This is one of the most important forest trees of Europe. It has been planted for reforestation in large numbers in many eastern and mid-western states.

Norway Spruce

Range: The Norway spruce is native to middle
Europe. It is the principal tree in the famous Black
Forest of Europe. It prefers rich, moist soil and is
rather tolerant of shade. It is found throughout the
Great Lakes region, primarily planted as an
ornamental tree.

White Cedar
Thuja occidentalis

The white cedar is one of the most widely planted evergreen trees in North America. It develops a conical symmetrical crown and usually reaches a height of 25 to 50 feet, and has a short trunk usually 1 to 2 feet in diameter.

The leaves are scale-like, ⅛ of an inch long, closely overlap one another, are aromatic when crushed and marked with glandular dots. They are arranged in pairs. Each succeeding pair alternates with the next pair.

The cones are oblong, ½ of an inch long, with 6 to 12 blunt-pointed, reddish-brown scales. The trunk usually divides near the base. The bark is grayish to reddish-brown, usually furrowed, and peels off into thin shred-like strips.

The white cedar prefers moist, shallow and rich soil with a limestone base, such as that found in the northern portions of the Great Lakes region. It has been planted widely for hedges and screens and various hybrids are used for ornamentation.

The wood of the white cedar is durable when in contact with the soil. It is also strong so it is often used for fence posts and roofs, and various garden construction projects. Lumber is generally not produced from this tree because of its relatively small size, yet it remains an important forest tree.

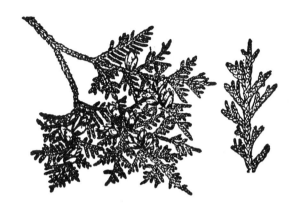

White Cedar

Range: The white cedar is found from southern Labrador west to Manitoba, Michigan, and Minnesota and south to North Carolina. It is common over the northern portions of the region, preferring low situations.

Red Cedar
Juniperus virginiana

Red cedar is a common household word. In recent years the red cedar chest has won its way to a special place in the modern home. It is believed that the beautiful wood also repels insects such as moths.

The leaves are of two kinds, namely, scale-shaped and awl-shaped. The scale-shaped are commonest, 1/16 of an inch long, closely pressed to twigs, and four ranked. The awl-shaped leaves are narrow, sharp-pointed, spreading, do not overlap, and occur in 2's and 3's.

The fruit is a dark blue berry about ¼ of an inch in diameter. Berries are freely eaten by birds.

The bark is very thin, reddish-brown, shallowly furrowed, peels off in long shred-lake strips.

The wood is soft, strong, very durable, of even texture and works easily. The heartwood is red and the sapwood is white. This color combination and its pronounced fragrance, account for its wide use in clothes closets and other interior wood work. In many parts of its range it is used for fence posts and in the manufacture of lead pencils.

The common juniper is closely related to the red cedar. It is a small, shrubby tree found locally in the Great Lake states. It rarely reaches tree size. Its awl-shaped leaves occur regularly in 3's.

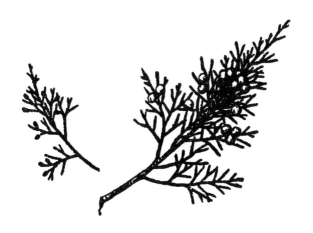

Red Cedar

Range: The red cedar is found from Nova Scotia to South Dakota south to Florida and Texas. In the Great Lakes region it is found primarily in the southern portions. This tree grows slowly and needs plenty of sunlight and rarely exceeds 50 feet in height and 18 inches in diameter. It has a distinctive narrow conical crown when growing in the open.

Black Willow

Salix nigra

The black willow reaches the largest size and has the widest distribution of any native American willow. It is the only native willow of timber size, sometimes reaching a height of 80 feet and a diameter of 4 feet.

It can always be distinguished by its simple, alternate, long, narrow, sharp-pointed leaves that are 3 to 5 inches long. At the base of the short leaf stalk are round leaf-like appendages that often clasp the twigs.

The flowers are of two different kinds. Both are arranged in short, stubby spikes. The pollen-bearing and seed-producing always occur on different trees. The seeds are minute, bear dense tufts of long, silky down, and occur in large numbers in small capsules on drooping tassels.

The bark varies from light brown to dark brown and black. On old trunks, it becomes furrowed and peels off in scales. The branches are slender, brittle, somewhat drooping. The buds are pointed, ½ of an inch long, and covered by a single reddish-brown scale.

The wood is pale, reddish-brown and is used chiefly in boxes, excelsior, charcoal, pulp, and certain wood working projects. It is not durable when in contact with the soil.

Black Willow

Range: The black willow occurs from New Brunswick to Florida, west to the Dakotas and southern Mexico. It is found throughout the Great Lakes region. It is often found in wet places but will grow in some dry situations. Branchlets carried down stream often catch in muddy banks and take root.

Pussy Willow
Salix discolor

The pussy willow, probably more than any other tree, tells people of both the city and country, when spring is here. During a brief period of spring, it gives the chief touch of beauty to the landscape through its fine display of yellow blossoms that are visited by thousands of bees.

The leaves are simple, alternate, elliptic, 3 to 5 inches long, bright green above and silvery white below. A distinctive feature of the leaves is the wavy margins with coarse teeth.

The flowers are of two kinds. Both are arranged in short, stubby spikes. The pollen-bearing and the seed-producing always occur on different trees. They appear before the leaves and tell us when spring is coming. The seeds are produced in large number in hairy, long-beaked, light-brown capsules.

The bark is thin, smooth, greenish, rarely scaly. The stout branchlets are marked with orange-colored breathing pores. The buds are alternate, ¼ of an inch long, duck-bill like, flattened on the inside, and dark reddish purple. The wood is similar to that of the black willow.

The pussy willow rarely exceeds 25 feet in height and is considerable value in landscape work, especially along water courses. It not only beautifies the stream banks but also prevents erosion.

Pussy Willow

Range: The pussy willow is found in moist meadows and along the banks of streams and in other wet places from Nova Scotia south to Delaware and est to Manitoba and Missouri. It is found throughout the Great Lakes region.

Sandbar Willow
Salix interior

What it lacks in height the sandbar willow makes up for in tenacity. The tree rarely exceeds 20 feet in height and resembles a woody shrub. But it is widely distributed where moist soil conditions are found. In particular, this is one of the first plants to stake a claim on barren, sandy soil found along beaches and riverbanks.

The leaves are linear to narrow lanceolate, firm, dentate, 2-6 inches long, and ⅛ to ½ of an inch wide. The leaves are somewhat curved and narrow at the base and acute at the apex with small and irregularly, wide-spaced teeth on the margin.

Twigs and branches are slender, orange to purplish-red and erect. Silky hairs are sometimes present. Branches are slender and flexible. The bark on old trunks is scaly.

The capsular fruit is round at the base and long-beaked.

This tree was sometimes planted as a windbreak but its rapid spread via roots make it objectionable in most circumstances.

Range: New Brunswick, east Quebec and Alaska to Maryland, Kentucky, Louisiana, Texas, Southeast New Mexico and east Montana. It is found throughout the Great Lakes region.

Introduced Willows

Three willows have been widely introduced into the Great Lakes region. They are the weeping willow, the white willow, and the crack willow.

The weeping willow (*Salix babylonica*), a native of Asia, was introduced into the U.S. in 1702 by a famous botanist named Tournefort. Sometimes this tree is called Napoleon willow because of its association with the great French general during his exile. It has been planted widely in the Great Lakes region.

This tree can always be distinguished by its weeping habit. Its long drooping branches are distinctive, and when young they are tough and pliable, but later become brittle. Its leaves are simple, alternate, 4 to 7 inches long; in shape they resemble the black willow and in color those of the white willow. The weeping willow is the most widely distributed of all introduced willows.

The white willow (*Salix alba*), a native of Europe, was brought to America by the early settlers. It is now found from the Atlantic Ocean to the Pacific and is given planting preference where erosion and landslides are to be stopped. It is found locally in the Great Lakes region as an ornamental tree. In some places it has escaped cultivation.

This tree sometimes reaches a height of 70 feet

and a diameter of 4 feet. The leaves are simple, alternate, 2 to 4 inches long, one-third to two-fifths of an inch wide, finely toothed along the edge. When young, the leaves are pale green and hairy on both sides, but when mature, they are distinctly white only on the lower surface, hence the name white willow.

The crack willow (*Salix fragilis*), a native of Europe and northern Asia, has been planted widely in America, especially in the prairie states. It is found throughout the Great Lakes states, particularly about the earlier settlements.

The crack willow (*Salix fragilis*), a native of Europe and northern Asia.

It is readily distinguished from the white willow by its yellowish-green twigs and larger leaves, which are 3 to 6 inches long, ½ to 1 inch wide, and coarsely toothed along the margin. The branches are so brittle that they crack off easily in a slight breeze, hence the appropriate name crack willow.

After a storm, the ground beneath this tree is often completely covered with twigs and branches.

Lombardy Poplar

Populus nigra italica

The Lombardy poplar is one of several introduced species of poplars found in the Great Lakes region.

The Lombardy popular is noted for is columnar form and was planted as a windbreak along some farmers' fields. Interestingly, it was planted near lighthouse and ports on the Great Lakes because sailors could distinguish them from a great distance at sea.

The tree grows 75 to 100 feet high, 1 to 30 feet in diameter, and has leaves that are rhombic-deltoid in shape. They are cuneate to truncate at the base. Leaves are 2 to 3½ inches long and 1½ to 3 inches wide. Twigs are slender, glabrous, yellowish and shining.

Buds are slightly resinous, conical, pointed, and glutinous. The bark is at first yellowish, later ash gray, ridged and dark brown on old trees and irregularly furrowed.

Because all trees planted in the U.S. have been staminate (pollen-producing) their range is strictly limited to where they have been planted. Look for them along coast lines as well as in open fields or around old residences in open areas.

The tree is native to Asia and is common in Italy.

Quaking Aspen
Populus tremuloides

The quaking aspen is also called trembling aspen and small-toothed aspen. The air must be remarkably still if the foliage is not quacking or trembling.

The flowers appear early in the spring. Pollen-bearing and seed-producing occur on different trees. Both are arranged in slender drooping tassels.

The fruit is a 2-valved capsule containing small seeds with tufts of fine hairs.

The bark is white or grayish to yellowish-green; on old trunks it becomes rough and black. The twigs are smooth, shiny, reddish-brown. The buds are narrow, conical, sharp-pointed, smooth, shiny, appear varnished, and are covered with 6 to 7 reddish-brown scales.

The wood is soft, weak, not durable, fine in texture, and white to light brown. It is used for paper pulp, boxes, crates, and wooden pallets.

One usually finds this tree associated with the large-toothed aspen and fire cherry on burnt-over and cut-over areas, where it springs up in large numbers. It reproduces freely from seeds, root shoots, and stump shoots. It grows rapidly and is short-lived. It soon makes a place for better trees and is generally called one of the "pioneer" species because it readily grows where no other trees will.

Quaking Aspen

Range: The quaking aspen is the most widely distributed tree in North America. It is a transcontinental tree extending from Newfoundland to Alaska and south to New Jersey, Kentucky, Mexico, and California. This tree is common throughout the region, especially in the northern portions.

Large-Toothed Aspen
Populus grandidentata

In spring, the large-toothed aspen is one of the most conspicuous trees of the forest. It is then that its pollen-bearing and seed-producing flowers dangle in long tassels from the tips of the twigs. The leaves are simple, alternate, broadly egg-shaped, 3 to 4 inches long, with coarse teeth along the margin. The leaf stalks are flattened laterally.

The flowers, like those of the quaking aspen, occur in drooping tassels. The pollen-bearing and seed-producing occur on different trees. The fruit is a 2-valved capsule in drooping tassels that become about 4 inches long.

The bark on old trunks is deeply furrowed and black. On upper parts of old trunks and young stems it is smooth, yellowish-green to white, and marked with black blotches. The twigs are rather stout, reddish to yellowish brown, often covered with a crusty coating, and sometimes peels in thin scales. The buds are ovate to conical, pointed, and covered with a dusty flour-like coating. They are not varnished. The wood is similar to that of the quaking aspen and is used the same.

It is common on cut-over and burnt-over lands. It sprouts freely from roots. It is short-lived and of little commercial value except that it prepares the soil for more valuable species to grow later.

Large-Toothed Aspen

Range: The large-toothed aspen is found from Nova Scotia and Ontario to Pennsylvania and along the mountains to North Carolina and west to Minnesota and Michigan. It is more common in the northern portions of the Great Lakes region.

White Poplar

Populus alba

The white poplar, also called silver leaf poplar, was widely planted after its introduction from Eurasia because it was thought to be a hardy shade and ornamental tree. After some time, however, tree lovers discovered that the tree had its shortcomings and is no longer recommended for yards and parks where it was planted.

The white poplar is a medium to large-size tree reaching 50 to 80 feet in height with a diameter of 2 to 3 feet. It forms a broad, rounded crown. Several trunks are often found together.

The leaves are ovate to triangular, 3 to 5 lobed or irregularly toothed. They are hairy at first to smooth on top with a distinctive white pubescence underneath. Leaves are usually 2 to 5 inches long and 1½ to 3½ inches wide with wavy or coarsely toothed margins. The leaf stem, like many other popular, is flattened.

The bud is white pubescent.

The bark is smooth on young trees, greenish white or gray, furrowed on old trunks and gray or dark brown. Shoots are common the near base and are generally white pubescent.

The wood is light, soft, and weak. It has no commercial value. It is often seen around older residences in the country.

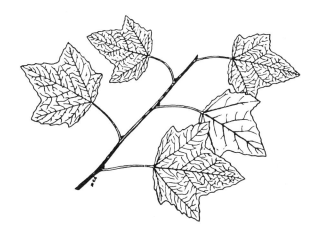

White Poplar

Range: Because it was introduced and widely planted as a shade and ornamental, it is found throughout the Great Lakes region. It is especially common on sandy, well-drained soils.

Cottonwood

Populus deltoides

The cottonwood, also called Carolina poplar, has been extensively planted along streets, in parks, and in yards in many places in the U.S.

The leaves are simple, alternate, broadly triangular, square at the base, 3 to 5 inches long, and have long and laterally flattened leaf-stalks. The flowers appear before the leaves. Pollen-bearing and seed-producing occur on different trees. Both are arranged in drooping tassels.

The fruit is a 3 to 4-valved capsule arranged in drooping tassels and contains numerous small seeds with tufts of fine hairs. The bark on young trunks is smooth and greenish-yellow, on old trunks it becomes ashy-gray to dark brown and deep furrowed. The lateral branches take an upright position. The twigs are stout, yellowish, marked with grayish dots, and have prominent ridges below leaf scars. The buds are large, resinous, glossy, and chestnut-brown. The terminal bud is often 5-angled.

The wood of the cottonwood is soft, not durable, white to brown, and works easily. It is used for paper pulp, boxes, crates, and pallets.

Because of its rapid growth the cottonwood gives immediate effects. It should not be planted along streets for it clogs sewers, lifts pavements, and has other undesirable habits.

Cottonwood

Range: The cottonwood is found from Quebec south to Florida and west to the Rocky Mountains. This tree is found throughout the Great Lakes region but is rare in the northern portions. It is easily propagated from cuttings.

Balsam Poplar

Populus balsamifera

The balsam poplar, also called the Balm of Gilead, is a well-known tree of the north woods where it reaches a height of 75 feet and a diameter of 3 feet.

The leaves are alternate, simple, ovate, 3 to 6 inches long, 1 to 3 inches wide, lustrous dark green above, and finely toothed along the margin. The leaf stalks are round and 1 to 2 inches long. The flowers appear in April before the leaves. The staminate (male, pollen-producing) are arranged in tassels 3 to 4 inches long and the pistillate (female, seed-producing) in loose-flowered tassels 4 to 5 inches long.

The fruit is a 2-valved capsule arranged in drooping tassels 4 to 5 inches long. It matures from May to June.

The bark on old trunks is thick, grayish, and roughened by shallow furrows and dark warty formations. The twigs are stout, reddish-brown to greenish-gray. The buds are large, long-pointed, sticky, resin-coated, and fragrant if crushed. The terminal bud is up to one inch long. The wood is light, soft, close grained, and light reddish-brown.

This tree prefers moist sites, river bottoms, and borders of lakes. It grows rapidly and is easily propagated from cuttings.

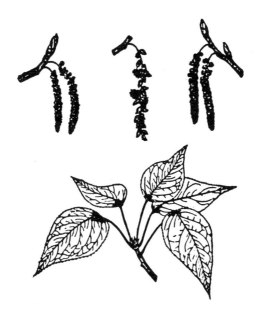

Balsam Poplar

Range: The balsam poplar is a tree of the north woods. It is found from Newfoundland south to New York and east through Michigan to Colorado and Alaska. In the Great Lakes states it is largest and most abundant in the northern portions.

Black Walnut

Juglans nigra

The black walnut is more fortunate than many trees in that it has only a few common names. Throughout its entire range of 650,000 square miles it is called walnut, black walnut, or walnut tree.

The leaves are alternate, compound, with 13 to 23 leaflets. Leaflets are 3 to 4 inches long, sharp-pointed, toothed along the margin, and stalkless.

The flowers are of two kinds. Both occur on the same tree. The pollen-bearing occur in unbranched drooping tassels. The nut-producing occur in few-flowered clusters on the new growth. The fruit is a round furrowed nut, 1 to 2 inches in diameter with a green, non-splitting fleshy husk which turns black when mature.

The bark is thick, rough, furrowed, dark brown to grayish-black. The twigs are stout, grayish-brown, bitter to taste, contain gray to light brown chambered pith. The buds are covered with downy scales. Terminal buds are as long as wide. Lateral buds are smaller. The wood is rich dark brown, hard, strong, splits easily, and very durable. It is used in furniture, interior finishings, gun stocks, and fine wood working.

It is not a good ornamental tree as its leaves appear late and drop early and it is often infested with caterpillars. It is difficult to transplant.

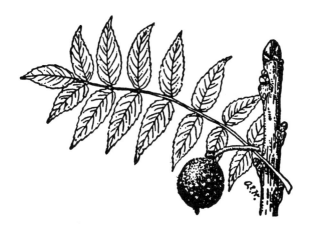

Black Walnut

Range: The black walnut is found from southern New England to Minnesota and south to Florida. This tree is found in the southern part of the Great Lakes region. The black walnut is an important timber tree, producing excellent lumber and fine nuts.

Butternut

Juglans cinerea

The butternut, also called white walnut, is a close kin of the black walnut.

The leaves are alternate, compound, with 13 to 23 leaflets.

The flowers are of two kinds. The pollen-bearing occur in unbranched drooping clusters. The nut-producing occur in few-flowered clusters on new growth.

The fruit is an elongated nut with a hairy, sticky husk. The nut is 4-ribbed, pointed at one end, sharply furrowed over the entire surface, and contains a sweet oily edible kernel.

The bark is gray to ashy-white, separates into wide flat ridges. The twigs are stout, greenish-gray, often downy, contain dark-brown chambered pith. The buds are covered with dense pale down. The terminal bud is ½ to ¾ of an inch long, flattened, blunt-pointed, and longer than wide. Lateral flower buds are pineapple-like, often placed one above another.

The wood is soft, not strong, light-brown. It is used in furniture, interior finishing, and fine wood working projects.

This tree prefers rich, moist soil and is often seen along streams, fences, and roads and rarely exceeds 50 feet in height and 2 feet in diameter.

Butternut

Range: The butternut is found from New Brunswick to Minnesota, south to Delaware and Arkansas and along the mountains to Georgia. It is common in the southern portions of the Great Lakes region.

Shagbark Hickory

Carya ovata

The shagbark hickory, or shellbark hickory, is the best-known of all the hickories. It produces the best nuts and has the most distinctive features of all the native hickories.

The leaves are alternate, 8 to 14 inches long, compound, with usually 5 leaflets. The three upper leaflets are the largest, the pair nearest the base is usually only about one-half the size of the terminal ones.

The flowers are similar to those of the other hickories.

The fruit is round, 1 to 1½ inches long, with husk that splits into 4 sections from apex to the base. The nuts are smooth, white, 4-angled, and pointed at the ends. The kernel is large and sweet.

The bark is smooth and light gray on young stems. On old trunks it becomes distinctly shaggy. The twigs are reddish-brown to gray, covered with numerous light dots, usually hairy. The buds are egg-shaped, blunt-pointed, about three-fifths of an inch long, and covered with about 10 bud scales.

The wood is very heavy, hard, strong, tough, elastic, and close-grained. It is used chiefly for handles and anywhere durability is required in fine woodwork. The nuts are prized by many forms of wildlife including deer, squirrels, and marmots.

Shagbark Hickory

Range: The shagbark hickory is found from
Quebec to Minnesota, south to Florida and Texas. It
is especially common in the southern portion of the
Great Lakes region. It usually reaches a height of
50 to 75 feet with a diameter of 2 feet.

Bitternut Hickory

Carya cordiformis

The bitternut hickory, also called swamp hickory and water hickory, is usually found in moist to wet locations. One usually finds it as a single specimen or in small groups in low and fertile situations in the rich agricultural valleys. It is the most handsome of the native hickories.

The leaves are alternate, compound, 6 to 10 inches long with 7 to 11 leaflets. Leaflets are long, narrow, sharp-pointed, and without stalks except the terminal one. They are smaller and slenderer than those of other hickories.

The flowers are of two kinds. They occur on the same tree. The pollen-bearing occur in drooping tassels, 3 to 4 inches long. The nut-producing occur in few-flowered clusters on new growth.

The fruit is a thin-shelled nut with a bitter kernel covered with a thin-shelled husk, which splits to the middle into 4 valves. Winged projections mark the meeting line of husk sections.

The bark is light gray, rather thin, roughened by shallow furrows, does not scale or shag off. The twigs are slender, smooth, grayish to orange brown or reddish. The buds are long, flattened, blunt-pointed, and covered by 4 yellowish scales.

The wood is heavy, hard, strong, and somewhat brittle.

Bitternut Hickory

Range: The bitternut hickory is found from Quebec to Minnesota, south to Florida and Texas. In the Great Lakes states it is most common in the southern portions. It may grow to a height of 100 feet with a 3-foot diameter. It grows best on rich, moist soil such as that found in a farm woodlot.

Pignut Hickory

Carya glabra

The pignut hickory is an important forest tree. It occurs on real forest soil on the foothills and mountain slopes, and produces valuable wood.

The leaves are alternate, compound, 8 to 12 inches long with 5 to 7 leaflets. Leaflets are long, narrow, sharp-pointed, smooth, and glossy. They are slightly larger than those of the bitternut hickory.

The flowers are similar to those of other hickories.

The fruit is pear-shaped to spherical, with a neck-like projection at the base. The husk is thin, often does not split or may split to the middle. The kernel is usually small and bitter and not edible.

The bark is close-fitting, dark gray, marked with shallow furrows, and does not shag off. The twigs are smooth, tough, reddish-brown, and marked with pale dots. The buds are oval, blunt-pointed, and reddish- brown.

The wood is similar to that of other hickories, but somewhat superior to the bitternut hickory.

Closely related to the pignut hickory is the mockernut hickory (*Carya alba*). It can be distinguished by its close-fitting, evidently furrowed bark that does not shag off. It has stout, hairy twigs and hairy leaves with 5 to 9 large leaflets. The buds are larger than those of any other hickory.

Pignut Hickory

Range: The pignut hickory is found from Maine to Minnesota, south to Florida and Texas. It occurs only in the southern portions of the Great Lake states. It is a medium-sized tree, frequently reaching a height of 60 feet and a diameter of 2 feet.

Paper Birch
Betula papyrifera

The paper birch is also called canoe birch and white birch. Every boy and girl has learned that the bark of this tree was used by the Indians and early settlers in the making of canoes and no person who has seen it will forget its chalky white bark.

The leaves are simple, alternate, oval, 2 or 3 inches long, and finely toothed on the margins.

The flowers appear about April and are of two kinds. The pollen-bearing occur in drooping tassels about 4 inches long. The seed-producing occur in small, erect spikes about 1 inch long.

The fruit is a short-stalked, usually drooping, cylindrical spike about 1½ inches long. The tiny seeds are winged and produced with 3-lobed scales.

The bark on older branches and small to medium stems is chalky to creamy white and peels off in thin papery scales marked with elongated yellowish-brown breathing pores. On old trunks it becomes rough and fissured. On very young stems it is golden to reddish-brown. When once removed, the bark is never renewed.

The wood is strong, hard, light-brown, with light sapwood. It is used for spools, fuel, paper pulp, and many common household articles.

This tree prefers wet situations such as stream banks and lake shores as well as rich uplands.

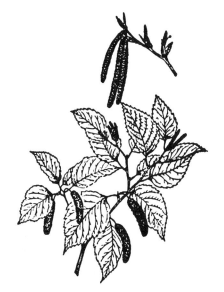

Paper Birch

Range: The paper birch is found in the north woods from the Atlantic Ocean to the Pacific. It extends east to Labrador, south to New Jersey and Pennsylvania and Michigan, west to the Rocky Mountains and from there to Alaska. It is especially common in the northern portions of the Great Lakes states. It may reach a height of 50 to 75 feet and a diameter of 3 feet.

Yellow Birch

Betula alleghaniensis

The yellow Birch is one of the largest deciduous trees of the northern U.S. It may reach a height of 100 feet and a diameter of 4 feet.

The leaves are alternate, simple, ovate, 3 to 4 inches long, wedge-shaped to heart-shaped at the base and doubly toothed along the margin.

The pollen-bearing flowers occur in tassels becoming 3 inches long; the seed-producing occur in small clusters about ⅔ of an inch long.

The fruit is an erect, cone-like strobile about 1 to 1½ inches long, made up of numerous 3-lobed scales bearing many tiny winged seeds.

The bark on young and middle-sized trees peels off in thin yellow film-like layers. On older trunks it becomes reddish-brown and rough and is without scales. The twigs are brown to silvery gray. The terminal twigs are long and slender; the lateral ones are short and stubby.

The wood is heavy, hard, strong, compact, but not durable. It is used for furniture, flooring, veneer, and fuel.

The yellow birch is found from Newfoundland to Pennsylvania, along the mountains to North Carolina and west to Minnesota. It is found throughout the region but is most common in the northern portions of its range.

Trees and Wildlife

Trees are the great provider for wild animals. Wildlife not only eats the nuts produced by oaks, walnuts, and hickories, but the seeds produced by birches, maples, and other trees.

These seeds are rich in oils that help deer, squirrels, chipmunks, mice, raccoons, and other animals survive long, cold winters in the Great Lakes area.

But trees provide more than food for wild animals. Holes in trees can be extensive and provide homes for bats, owls, raccoons, squirrels, chipmunks, flying squirrels, opossums, and others.

On a forest walk look above you and you may discover that trees provide nesting places for birds as well. Some birds, such as robins, prefer nests that are relatively close to the ground so look between the branches of spruce trees to find their nests hidden from danger.

Some birds, such as crows and hawks, prefer nests that overlook the forest so they can flee before danger arrives. Masses of twigs and leaves can be found in the crowns of tall maples, oaks, and beech.

Finally, the forests also provide soil and light conditions suitable for a host of other plants that provide additional food and shelter for wild animals.

Next time you are in a forest, look up and see if you can spot the value of trees to wildlife!

Eastern Hophornbeam

Ostrya virginiana

The hophornbeam, also called ironwood, has appropriate common names as its fruit is hop-like and the wood is "hard as iron."

It is the only tree native to eastern North America that produces hop-like fruit. An examination of the fruit shows that it is made up of a number of loose papery bags in each of which is found a little brown nutlet.

The seed bags are arranged in clusters usually from 1 to 2 inches long and attached to the twig by a hairy stem.

The leaves are simple, alternate, 3 to 5 inches long, ovate, long-pointed, and finely toothed along the margin.

The flowers are of two kinds. Pollen-bearing and seed-producing occur on the same tree. The former occur in drooping tassels about 2 inches long, and the latter are produced in erect clusters. During the winter the partly developed pollen-bearing flower catkins occur in clusters of 3 or 4 at the ends of the twigs.

The twigs are very delicate and interlacing. The thin grayish brown bark peels off in narrow, flat scales and is also helpful in recognizing this tree. The small, reddish-brown buds with four-ranked bud scales are distinctive.

Eastern Hophornbeam

Range: The hophornbeam is widely distributed over the eastern U.S. It is found from Cape Breton Island to Florida and west to Minnesota and Texas. This tree, usually found solitary, is common throughout the Great Lakes region. It rarely grows larger than 30 feet high and 12 inches in diameter.

American Hornbeam

Carpinus caroliniana

The American hornbeam, also called ironwood, blue beech, and water beech, is a small, bushy tree usually found along streams and other low places. In appearance it will pass for a little brother of the beech.

The leaves are simple, alternate, 2 to 4 inches long, ovate, long pointed, and finely toothed along the margin.

The flowers are of two kinds, both appearing on the same tree. The pollen-bearing occur in tassels about 1½ inches long; the seed-producing in few-flowered clusters about ¾ of an inch long.

The fruit is a small, prominently ribbed nut about one-third of an inch long, enclosed in a leaf-like 3-lobed bract, which is usually toothed on one margin of the middle lobe. The seed is attached to a leaf-like bract.

The bark is thin, smooth, bluish-green, and marked with distinctive furrows running up and down along the trunk. The twigs are slender, reddish to orange, and covered with scattered pale breathing pores. Small buds are about ⅛ of an inch long, covered with 8 to 12 reddish-brown bud scales.

The wood is heavy, hard, and strong. It is sometimes used for handles but is of little value.

American Hornbeam

Range: The American hornbeam is found from
Nova Scotia to Florida and west to Minnesota and
Texas. In the Great Lakes region it is most common
in the southern portions where it sometimes is
found in dense masses.

Smooth Alder

Alnus rugosa

The smooth alder, also called black alder, is one of the commoner woody plants found along the streams and in other wet places of the Great Lakes region. It usually remains a shrub but sometimes grows to a height of 20 feet.

The leaves are simple, alternate, obovate, rounded at the apex, wedge-shaped at the base, and have a finely toothed margin.

The flowers appear before the leaves and are of two kinds. The pollen-bearing occur in drooping tassels 2 to 5 inches long. The seed-producing are greenish to purplish with scarlet styles. They are about ¼ of an inch long and occur in 2's or 3's at the end of the branches.

The fruit is a cone-like woody structure about ½ to ¾ of an inch long.

The bark is thin, smooth, often grooved, grayish-green, dotted with numerous brown lenticels, and marked with white blotches. The twigs are greenish to grayish brown, with 3 bundle scars. The buds are alternate, ½ of an inch long, evidently stalked, blunt-pointed, and covered with 2 scales.

The wood is yellowish-brown and marked with broad rays. Although it rarely reaches tree size, it is helpful in preventing erosion along stream banks.

Smooth Alder

Range: The smooth alder is found from Maine to Florida and Texas and west to Minnesota. It is common throughout the Great Lakes region.

Chestnut
Castanea dentata

This tree was once common and provided nuts
for traditional Christmas celebrations. A fungus
blight, however, has killed most of these trees in the
region. All that are left in many areas are suckers
growing from stumps.

The leaves are simple, alternate, 6 to 8 inches
long, sharp-pointed, and coarsely toothed.

The flowers appear in June or July. They are
arranged in slender, yellowish-white pencil-like
plumes. Pollen-bearing flowers make up most of
these plumes. The seed-producing flowers occur in
small numbers near the base of the plumes.

The fruit is a prickly bur with 1 to 5 nuts
maturing in September or October.

The bark on branches and small trunks is
smooth, brownish, and close-fitting; on old trunks it
becomes grayish-brown and deeply furrowed.

The twigs are smooth, greenish to brown, dotted
with numerous small white breathing pores. The
buds are alternate, ¼ of an inch long, blunt-pointed
and covered with 2 to 3 chestnut brown scales.

The wood is light, soft, not strong, coarse-
grained, and durable. It is used for fine wood
working. Chestnut trees of commercial size, with
few exceptions, have been wiped out by the fungus
blight.

Chestnut

Range: The chestnut is found from Maine to Michigan, and south to the Carolinas and Georgia and Arkansas. It is found only in the southernmost portions of the Great Lakes region.

American Beech

Fagus grandifolia

No hardwood tree is more beautiful or more easily recognized than the American beech.

The leaves are simple, alternate, 3 to 4 inches long, pointed at the tip, wedge-shaped at the base, and coarsely-toothed along the margin. When mature, they are stiff, leathery, with straight, sunken veins. The flowers are of two kinds and appear about April. The pollen-bearing occur in stalked round heads; the nut-producing in a few-flowered clusters.

The fruit is a stalked, prickly, four-valved bur, usually produced in pairs, containing triangular, pale brown, shining nutlets with a sweet kernel.

The bark is smooth, light gray. The twigs are slender, dark gray, and marked with circles of bud-scale scars. The buds are alternate, slender, conical, sharp-pointed, ¾ inch long, 5 times as long as wide, and covered with 10 to 20 reddish-brown scales.

The wood is very hard and strong. It is an excellent fuelwood and is used extensively in the manufacture of charcoal, and chemicals.

The American beech is desirable for landscaping on account of its clean trunk, fine crown, deep shade and freedom from insect attack. It deserves to be classed among our most beautiful forest trees.

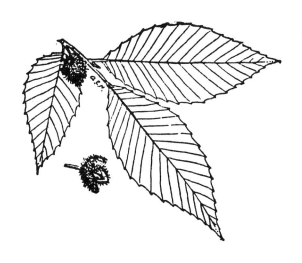

American Beech

Range: The American beech is found from Nova Scotia to Wisconsin and south to Florida. This tree is common throughout Michigan, especially in the hardwood forests of the north. It is hardy throughout its range and prefers deep, rich and well-drained soil.

White Oak

Quercus alba

The white oak is the most important hardwood forest tree native to North America. The original forests of the rich agricultural areas of the U.S. were largely made up of this great tree.

The leaves are simple, alternate, 5 to 9 inches long, 2 to 4 inches wide. They are divided into 3 to 9, usually 7, blunt-pointed, finger-like lobes. Mature leaves are dark green above and light green beneath.

The fruit is a sessile or shore-stalked acorn maturing in one season. The light brown nuts are about ¾ inch long, seated in a warty cup, enclosing about ¼ of the nut. The nuts are relished by wildlife.

The bark is grayish-white and peels off in numerous loose scales. The early settlers made it into a tea used in the treatment of tonsillitis. The twigs are smooth, light gray, and dotted with light lenticels.

The buds are alternate, egg-shaped, blunt-pointed, reddish brown, and clustered at the end of twigs.

The wood is heavy, hard, strong, close-grained, light-brown, and durable. Its uses are interior finishing, flooring, furniture, general construction, and fuel.

White Oak

Range: The white oak is found from Maine to
Minnesota and south to Florida. It is common
throughout southern Michigan, becoming rarer
northward, especially in the upper peninsula. This
tree reaches its best development on rich, moist soil,
where it attains a height of 75 to 100 feet and 2 to
4 feet in diameter.

Swamp White Oak

Quercus bicolor

The swamp white oak is usually found in swamps, about ponds, and along the banks of streams. In youth, it is rather attractive, but with advancing years it becomes ragged and unkempt in appearance.

The leaves are simple, alternate, 5 to 6 inches long, 3 to 4 inches broad, wavy-toothed on the margin, dark green above, and light green and hairy on the lower surface. They are broadest between the middle and the apex.

The flowers and wood are similar to those of the white oak.

The fruit is a long-stalked acorn that matures in one season. The acorns are about an inch long and usually occur in pairs.

The bark on old trunks is thick, grayish-brown and breaks in long deep furrows. On the small branches it sheds off in flakes like that of the sycamore. The twigs are stout, yellowish to reddish-brown. The buds are about ⅛ of an inch long, blunt-pointed, smooth, and reddish-brown.

Trees 2 to 4 feet in diameter and 80 feet high are not unusual. The largest ever recorded was the Wadsworth Oak of New York, which was 27 feet in circumference.

Swamp White Oak

Range: The swamp white oak is found from Maine to Michigan and south to Georgia and Arkansas. This tree is found in the rich, moist soil bordering swamps and streams in the southern portion of the region.

Bur Oak

Quercus macrocarpa

The bur oak, also called mossy cup oak and over cup oak, is one of the largest of American oaks. It often reaches a height of 100 feet and 4 to 5 feet in diameter.

The leaves are simple, alternate, 6 to 12 inches long, 3 to 6 inches wide, shiny and deep green above, and pale and finely hairy beneath. Near the middle are deep clefts that almost divide the leaves in two parts.

The flowers and wood are similar to those of white oak.

The fruit is a large acorn maturing in one season. The nuts are ¾ of an inch long with a white and sweet kernel. The cup covers about half of the nut and is bordered by a distinct fringe along the margin.

The twigs are stout, yellowish-brown, and usually marked with corky winged projections. The buds are alternate, ⅛ of an inch long, blunt-pointed, reddish-brown, and clustered at the end of twigs. The bark becomes deeply furrowed and has a tendency to peel off in flaky scales.

The bur oak is a valuable timber tree and is used somewhat for ornamental planting. It is easy to transplant and grows rapidly and has few insect enemies. The wood is used for veneer and furniture.

Bur Oak

Range: The bur oak has a very wide range as it is found from New Brunswick and Nova Scotia west to Manitoba, and south to Pennsylvania, Kansas and Texas. It is common throughout the region.

Chinquapin Oak

Quercus muhlenbergii

The chinquapin oak, also called sweet oak, yellow oak, and chestnut oak, was a favorite tree among the pioneers who sought it for fence posts because of its durability.

The leaves are simple, alternate, 4 to 8 inches long, taper-pointed at the apex, smooth and dark green above, and grayish, hairy beneath with coarsely toothed margins divided by more or less incurved teeth.

The flowers are similar to those of the white oak.

The fruit is an acorn, generally stalkless and maturing in one season. The nut is ovoid, ½ to 1 inch long, enclosed for about ½ its length by a thin cup covered with brown woolly scales.

The bark is grayish-brown. The twigs are slender, reddish-brown, at first hairy but become smooth. The buds are chestnut brown, sharp-pointed, about 1/6 of an inch long. The wood is similar to that of the white oak. It is used for veneer and furniture as well as fine wood working.

The chinquapin oak was a favorite of the passenger pigeon before the bird became extinct. Its fruit is the most edible of all the oaks.

The tree prefers limestone soil and is frequently found on dry hillsides and on rocky river banks.

Chinquapin Oak

Range: The chinquapin oak is found from Vermont to Minnesota and south to Florida and Texas. This tree is found naturally only in the southern portions of the region.

Red Oak

Quercus rubra

The red oak is one of the biggest, stateliest, and handsomest trees of eastern North America.

The leaves are simple, alternate, 5 to 9 inches long, 4 to 6 inches wide, and 7 to 9-lobed. Lobes are bristle-tipped and reach halfway to the midrib.

The flowers appear with the leaves. The pollen-bearing flowers are arranged in drooping tassels; the acorn-producing occur in few-flowered clusters on new growth.

The fruit is an acorn maturing in two seasons. The cup is wide, shallow, covered with over-lapping reddish-brown scales enclosing only the base of the nut. The nuts average one inch long and ½ to ¾ of an inch wide, and are flat at the base and short-tipped at the apex.

The bark on young stems is smooth, grayish or brown. On older trunks it becomes rough with furrows separating wide, smooth grayish to brownish ridges. The lateral branches are straight and ascend at about an angle of 45 degrees. The twigs are smooth and rich brown. The buds are ¼ of an inch long, sharp-pointed, smooth, glossy, reddish-brown, and without hairs.

The wood is heavy, hard, strong, light reddish-brown, with light sapwood. It is used for furniture, interior finishing, and veneer.

Red Oak

Range: The red oak has a wide distribution. It is
found from Nova Scotia to Minnesota and Kansas
south to Florida and Texas. It is most often found
in the southern portions of the Great Lakes region.
It may reach a height of 150 feet and an age of 300
years or more.

Black Oak

Quercus velutina

The black oak is one of the largest oaks native to the eastern states. It reaches a height of 100 feet and 4 feet in diameter. By its bark, one can always recognize this tree. Its outer bark is black and its inner bark is distinctly yellow.

The leaves are simple, alternate, 4 to 10 inches long, 3 to 6 inches wide, and usually 7-lobed with bristle tips. The lower leaf surfaces are pale green to rusty brown.

The flowers are similar to those of other oaks (see red oak).

The fruit is an acorn maturing in two seasons. Cups are cup-shaped, light brown, often slightly fringed along the margin, and enclose half of the nut. Nuts are ½ to 1 inch long, light reddish-brown.

The bark on older trunks is black, thick, and very rough. Twigs are stout, angular, reddish-brown, and often hairy. Buds are large, sometimes ½ of an inch long, angular, and covered with a coating of yellowish or dirty-white hairs.

The wood is similar to that of red oak and is used extensively for furniture making and veneer. The wood of the black oak is sometimes used interchangeably with red oak.

The black oak usually grows on dry uplands and gravelly plains. It prefers glacial drift areas.

Black Oak

Range: The black oak is found from Maine to Ontario, and south to Florida and Texas. It occurs throughout the southern portions of the Great Lakes states.

Scarlet Oak

Quercus coccinea

The scarlet oak, is among the showiest of the American oaks. Its autumn garb of brilliant scarlet red and crimson makes it stand out among all its associates. This coloration does not develop in all parts of its natural range.

The leaves are simple, alternate, 3 to 6 inches long, 3 to 5 inches wide, and 5 to 9-lobed. Lobes are bristle-tipped and separated by deep clefts.

The flowers resemble those of other oaks.

The fruit is an acorn maturing in two seasons. The cup is thin, narrowed at the base, often glossy on the surface, and covers ½ of the nut. The nut is three-fifths of an inch long and reddish-brown.

The bark on small stems and branches is smooth, thin, light to grayish-brown and becomes rough and irregular on older trunks, sometimes almost black near the base. Flat-topped ridges occur between shallow furrows. The inner bark is of a pale coloring. Dead limbs often persist along the lower trunk. The twigs are smooth, rather slender, reddish to grayish-brown. The buds are about ¼ of an inch long and covered with a pale wool from apex to the middle.

The wood is rather strong, heavy, hard, and coarse in texture. It does not have wide commercial use. It is sometimes used for fuel.

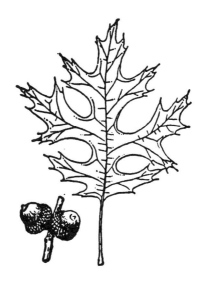

Scarlet Oak

Range: The scarlet oak is found from Maine to
Minnesota south to North Carolina and west to
Nebraska. It occurs over the lower peninsula of
Michigan. It grows on dry, sandy soils as well as
moist foothills. It is planted extensively as an
ornamental because of its fall coloration.

Pin Oak

Quercus palustris

The pin oak is one of the most attractive oaks native to the Great Lakes region. Its trunk usually remains unbranched and the lateral branches take a horizontal position along the middle of the trunk. At the bottom they are drooping and those at the tip are ascending.

The leaves are simple, alternate, 4 to 6 inches long, 2 to 4 inches wide, 5 to 9 lobed. Lobes are bristle-tipped and separated by deep clefts. They resemble those of the scarlet oak but are coarser and less lustrous.

The fruit is a tiny acorn, maturing in two seasons. The cup is thin, shallow, saucer-shaped, about ½ inch across. The nut is light brown, often striped, about ½ inch long.

The bark is smooth, grayish or dark brown. The twigs are smooth, shiny, grayish-brown. The branches are thickly set with stiff pin-like twigs, which is how the name was derived. The buds are small, smooth, light brown.

The wood is heavy, hard, and strong. It is used for fuel and general construction. The pin oak is a medium-sized tree, reaching a height of 75 feet and a diameter of 3 feet. It grows rapidly and is well adapted for shade, park, and street planting. The wood is used for fuel and general construction.

Pin Oak

Range: The pin oak is found from Massachusetts to
Michigan and south to Georgia. Rich bottomlands
are its favorite home.

Shingle Oak
Quercus inbricaria

The shingle oak, also called laurel oak, peach oak, jack oak and water oak, is among the unique oaks of North America. At first glance it appears to be an oversize laurel because of its laurel-like leaves, but a close examination reveals acorns, placing it definitely among the oaks.

The leaves are simple, alternate, 4 to 6 inches long, 1 to 2 inches wide, wedge-shaped at the base, sharp-pointed at the apex, and smooth along the margin.

The flowers are similar to those of the red oak.

The fruit is a small acorn maturing in two seasons. The nut is egg-shaped about ½ of an inch long and dark brown. The cup is saucer-shaped, reddish-brown, and encloses almost half the nut.

The bark is light to grayish-brown and becomes rough with shallow furrows. On young trunks it is smooth and shiny. The twigs are smooth, shiny, and dark brown. The buds are about ⅛ of an inch long and chestnut-brown.

The wood is rather heavy, hard and strong. It is similar to red oak but somewhat inferior.

The shingle oak may reach a height of 80 feet and a diameter of 3 feet. It has an attractive form and beautiful foliage, which makes it preferred for ornamental planting.

Shingle Oak

Range: The shingle oak is found from
Pennsylvania to Michigan, south to Georgia and
Arkansas. This unique oak tree is relatively rare in
the Great Lakes region and occurs in both moist
and upland conditions.

American Elm

Ulmus americana

Of all trees native to North America, the American elm is probably the best known and most admired. For beauty, grace, and stateliness, this tree has no superior.

The leaves are simple, alternate, 4 to 6 inches long, and unequally based. The veins run straight from the midrib to the doubly=toothed margins.

The flowers appear in the spring before the leaves. They are greenish and hang in clusters.

The fruit is a small seed, surrounded completely by a thin, flat, membrane-like wing. It matures after the flowers and is about ½ of an inch across.

The bark is grayish-brown, rather thick, roughened by shallow furrows, sometimes flaky or corky. The twigs are smooth, reddish-brown, and marked with obscure pale breathing pores. The leaf scars are marked with three distinct bundle-scars. The buds are egg-shaped, usually smooth, covered with 6 to 10 overlapping reddish-brown scales with darker margins.

The wood is heavy, hard, tough, rather durable, dark brown to red with lighter sapwood. It is used for small wood working projects.

This tree has been affected by the Dutch elm disease, which makes it unusual to find large specimens.

American Elm

Range: The American elm has a total range of
more than 2,500,000 square miles. It extends from
Newfoundland west to the Rocky Mountains, a
distance of 3,000 miles, and south to Florida and
Texas, a distance of 1,200 miles. It is common
throughout the Great Lakes region.

Slippery Elm
Ulmus fulva

The slippery elm, also called red elm and moose elm, has been a well-known tree ever since the pioneer hunters and early travellers learned that its bark has excellent properties for quenching thirst and staying hunger. The bark is still held in esteem for folk remedies for sore throats, fevers, and inflammations.

The leaves are simple, alternate, 5 to 7 inches long, rough, unequally based, and doubly toothed on the margins.

The greenish flowers appear early in the spring before the leaves. They occur in few-flowered clusters along twigs.

The fruit is a small seed surrounded completely by a thin, flat, membrane-lake wing. It is about ½ of an inch across and matures shortly after the flowers.

The bark is dark brown tinged with red and becomes rough and furrowed. The inner bark is slippery, fragrant, and mucilaginous. The twigs are grayish and rather rough when mature. The buds are dark chestnut-brown and covered with about 12 hairy, rusty-brown scales.

The wood is heavy, hard, tough, dark brown to red with light sapwood. The wood is used for a variety of wood working projects.

Slippery Elm

Range: The slippery elm is found from the Valley of the St. Lawrence, south to Florida and west to North Dakota and Texas. It occurs frequently throughout the Great Lakes region along stream banks, bottomlands, and moist hillsides.

Rock Elm

Ulmus racemosa

The rock elm, also called hickory elm, sometimes reaches a height of 100 feet and a diameter of 5 feet.

The leaves are alternate, simple, 3 to 6 inches long, coarsely toothed along the margin, unequally based, and thick and firm in texture.

The flowers appear in March and April before the leaves, in slender-stalked, drooping, raceme-like clusters.

The fruits matures in May. It is a small, one-seeded samara surrounded with a thin membranous wing about half an inch long and hairy all over.

The bark on the main trunk is thick, ridged with wide furrows separating fly scaly ridges. The twigs are at first light brown and hairy and become shiny reddish-brown and finally grayish-brown with corky winged projections. The buds are alternate, egg-shaped, brownish, and a quarter of an inch long with minutely hairy bud scales.

The wood is heavy, very strong, tough, light reddish-brown with light sapwood. It is used for purposes requiring toughness, solidity, and flexibility.

This tree prefers a rich, well-drained soil and can grow large in glaciated areas.

Rock Elm

Range: The rock elm is found from Quebec, westward to Ontario, Michigan, and Wisconsin and northeast Nebraska and southward through the New England states to New York and central Indiana. It is especially common in the southern portions of its range.

Hackberry
Celtis occidentalis

The hackberry, also called sugarberry, nettle-tree, and hack-tree, is not a common tree in the Great Lakes region.

The leaves are simple, alternate, ovate, 2 to 4 inches long, finely toothed along the margins, sharp-pointed, rounded and often lopsided at the base, and rough on the upper surfaces with prominent primary veins.

The flowers are small, greenish and borne on slender stalks. The fruit is a round, dark purple berry about ¼ of an inch in diameter. It matures about September, hangs far into the winter, and is eaten readily by birds and other animals.

The grayish brown bark ranges from smooth, like that of the beech, to very rough. Hard wart-like bark projections are common on medium-sized trees. The twigs are slender, tend to zigzag, and are often grouped in dense clusters known as "witches' brooms." They contain a pith that is made up of thin white plates separated by wide air spaces. This is known as "chambered pith."

The wood is yellowish, rather heavy, and coarse-grained. It is used for crates, handles, and a variety of wood working projects.

The hackberry rarely exceeds 50 feet and prefers rich, moist soil near streams.

Hackberry

Range: The hackberry has a wide distribution. It is found from New England to the Pacific coast and south to Florida and Texas. It is most commonly found in the southern portions of the Great Lakes region.

Red Mulberry

Morus rubra

The red mulberry, also known as black mulberry and more frequently called "mulberry," came in the limelight in the early days of American history when it was wrongly supposed as a food for silkworms.

The leaves are simple, alternate, 3 to 5 inches long, roundish, short-tipped, deep green and with deeply sunken veins on the upper surface. Some leaves are lobed and resemble an ordinary mitten. Leaf stalks give a milky secretion when squeezed.

The flowers are of two kinds. Pollen-bearing and seed-producing occur in short drooping tassels.

The fruit is a soft, fleshy, dark red to black aggregation of many-seeded berries. They are sweet, juicy, and greatly relished by man, birds, and various other animals.

The bark is rather thin, dark, grayish brown, begins to roughen about the third year, and peels off in thin scales. The twigs are smooth, clean, light greenish-brown, and bear oval, hollowed-out leave scars dotted with numerous bundler scars. The bowl-shaped leaf scars are helpful in recognizing this tree in the winter.

The wood is soft, light, not strong, orange yellow to brown. It is durable in contact with the soil and used for fence posts.

Red Mulberry

Range: The red mulberry, which rarely exceeds 50 feet in height and 2 feet in diameter, is the only mulberry native to North America. It grows from Massachusetts west to Kansas and south to Texas and Florida. It is found in the southern portions of the Great Lakes region. Rich, moist soil of river bottoms, valleys, and foothills is its favorite home.

Osage Orange

Maclura pomifera

The osage orange is often referred to as "cantankerous" because of its thorny, intertwining branches. Because of this characteristic it was often planted along fencerows to keep cows from wandering beyond its borders.

The leaves of the osage orange are dark, shiny green, simple, alternate, have wavy, untoothed margins. When squeezed, the leaves exude a thick, bitter juice.

The bark is tan, deeply furrowed with shreddy, interlacing ridges and the trunk often divides near the ground. Twigs are dotted with orange lenticels and contain an orange pith. Twigs are also armed with spines that are ¾ of an inch long.

Pollen-producing flowers and fruit-producing flowers are found on separate trees. The pollen-producing flowers are green, in spikes, 1 to 1½ inches long. The fruit-producing flowers are dense, round and drooping heads on short stalks.

The fruit resembles a pale green orange, 3 to 5 inches in diameter with a warty exterior. Inside are a series of seed sacks with a brown nutlet.

The wood is durable and extremely strong. It was the preferred wood for carving bows by American Indians. There are no current uses for the wood and it is of no economic importance today.

Osage Orange

Range: The osage orange is not particularly common anywhere but is found throughout much of the Great Lakes region, especially along fence rows. It may grow 50 to 60 feet high and 2 to 3 feet in diameter.

Tulip Tree

Liridendron tulipifera

The tulip tree, also called yellow poplar and whitewood, is one of the most distinctive of American trees.

The leaves are simple, alternate, usually 4-lobed, 4 to 6 inches across, appear to have tips cut off at right angles to the stem, and are long-stalked. At the base of each leafstalk are two leaf appendages. The flowers are tulip-like 1½ to 2 inches deep, greenish-yellow with 3 reflexed sepals and 6 petals.

The fruit is made up of long-winged nutlets arranged in light brown, cone-like clusters 2½ to 3 inches long.

The bark, when young, is smooth, bitter, ashy-gray to brown and mottled with light blotches. On old trunks, it is thick, brown, and deeply furrowed. The twigs are smooth, shiny, stout, reddish-brown, and marked with pale obscure breathing pores. Complete rings of stipule scars surround twigs.

The buds are smooth, flattened, ¼ to ½ of an inch long, blunt-pointed, reddish-brown, and covered with one pair of bud scales. Within buds are small miniature leaves.

The wood is soft, not strong, light, white-yellowish to brownish, and work easily.

Deep, rich, moist soil is its favorite home and frequently reaches a height of 80 feet.

Tulip Tree

Range: The tulip tree is found from Rhode Island to Michigan, south to Florida and Arkansas. It is most commonly found in the southern portion of the region but is becoming more common as an ornamental planting.

Sassafras

Sassafras variifolium

The sassafras, also called sassafrac and saxifrax, is a distinctive tree. It is recorded that sassafras bark and roots were among the first cargo shipped from the American colonies. The bark and roots are still used in some areas for making sassafras tea.

The leaves are simple, alternate, egg-shaped, 4 to 6 inches long, and usually smooth along the margin. Sometimes 2 to 5-lobed leaves are found on the same twig with the normal leaves. The glove form of leaves are distinctive.

The flowers appear with the leaves and are of two kinds. They are greenish-yellow, and arranged in loose, short-stalked clusters.

The fruit is a dark blue, shiny berry borne on a stout red stem. It is excellent bird food.

The bark becomes rough early. On old trunks it is reddish-brown, deeply furrowed, and separates in thin scales. The twigs are rather brittle, yellowish-green, aromatic, and sometimes hairy. The inner bark is very mucilaginous. The buds are about 3/5 of an inch long, slightly hairy, greenish, and covered with a few bud scales.

The wood is soft, brittle, durable, aromatic, dull orange-brown, with light sapwood. It is used for many wood working projects as well as posts, furniture, and interior finishing.

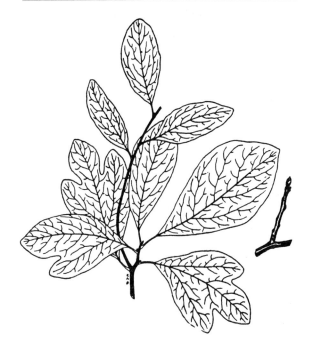

Sassafras

Range: The sassafras is found from Massachusetts to Florida and west to Michigan and Texas. It is often found in the southern portions of the Great Lakes states. It prefers well-drained, stony or sandy soil. It is common in abandoned fields.

Witch Hazel

Hamamelis virginiana

The witch hazel is a very interesting small tree. It has the unusual habit of blossoming late in autumn and a full year elapses between the appearance of its flowers and the maturing of its unusual fruit.

The leaves are simple, alternate, oval, 4 to 6 inches long, usually rounded at the apex, oblique at the base and coarsely toothed along the margin with prominent veins.

The flowers appear in October or November. They are bright yellow and occur in few-flowered clusters.

The fruit ripens in October or November with the flowers. It is a yellowish-brown woody pod with two cells in which black shiny seeds are produced. The seeds are often propelled five or more feet when seed pods burst open.

The bark is light brown, somewhat mottled with light blotches. The twigs are light brown, smooth, zigzag. The buds are flattish, curved, brown, and hairy. The terminal bud is sickle-shaped, about ⅓ of an inch long. Flower buds are small, round, and occur on slender stalks.

The wood is hard, light brown, and close grained. It is not used commercially. This tree prefers moist and rocky situations.

Witch Hazel

Range: Witch hazel is found from Nova Scotia to Minnesota, south to Florida and Texas. It is common throughout the Great Lakes region but rarely reaches tree size.

Sycamore
Platanus occidentalis

The sycamore, also called buttonball, button wood, and plane tree, is the largest tree of Michigan.

The leaves are simple, alternate, broadly ovate, 3 to 5 lobed, 4 to 10 inches across, bright green above and pale green and white woolly below. The leave stalks are about 2 inches long, enlarged and hollowed at the base.

The flowers are of two kinds, occur in dense ball-like heads attached to twigs by long slender stalks.

The fruit consists of tiny seeds, arranged in ball-like heads about 1 inch in diameter. They are attached to twigs by long slender stalks.

The bark on old trunks is rather thick, dark brown and peels off in broad scales. On young stems and the upper part of larger trunks, it peels off in thin scales exposing white, greenish and yellowish inner bark. The twigs are rather stout, at first green and fuzzy, later grayish to brown and smooth. The buds are about ¼ of an inch long, conical, dull-pointed, smooth, and reddish-brown. The terminal bud is absent.

The wood is hard, strong, reddish-brown. It is used for boxes, furniture, novelties, charcoal, and chemicals.

Sycamore

Range: The sycamore is native from Maine to
Minnesota and south to Florida and Texas. Moist to
wet fertile soil are its favorite home. It is primarily
found in the southern portions of the region.

Wild Black Cherry

Prunus serotina

The wild black cherry, also called wild cherry, black cherry, and cabinet cherry, is the only native cherry that reaches large tree size. It often attains a height of 75 feet and a diameter of 3 feet.

The leaves are simple, alternate, 2 to 5 inches long, long-pointed, finely toothed along the margin, rather thick, shiny on the upper surface and paler below with a brown pubescence along the midrib.

The flowers are white, about ¼ of an inch across, and arranged in spikes 3 to 4 inches long.

The fruit is a purplish-black juicy berry, about ⅓ of an inch in diameter and grouped in drooping clusters.

The bark on young trunks is smooth, glossy, reddish-brown marked with conspicuous white, horizontally elongated breathing pores and peels off in thin film-like layers exposing green inner bark. On old trunks it becomes black, rough, and breaks up into plates. To some, the bark of old trees appears as burnt potato chips glued to the trunk.

Twigs are smooth, reddish-brown and marked with numerous small whitish breathing pores. The buds are about ⅛ of an inch long, smooth, glossy, reddish-brown, and covered with about 4 visible scales.

The wood is prized for furniture and paneling.

Wild Black Cherry

Range: The wild black cherry is found from Nova Scotia south to Florida and west to Kansas and Texas. It is common in the southern portions of the Great Lakes region.

Pin Cherry

Prunus pennsylvanica

The pin cherry is a small, slender tree seldom more than 30 feet high and 12 inches in diameter.

The leaves are alternate, sometimes paired but never opposite each other. They are simple, 3 to 5 inches long and ¾ to 1¼ inches wide, finely toothed along the margin, and bright green and shiny on upper surfaces and paler below.

The flowers appear about May when leaves are partly developed. They are white, about ½ inch across and arranged in 4 to 5-flowered clusters. The fruit is a round, juicy, light red berry, about ¼ of an inch in diameter. The skin is thick and the flesh sour. It ripens in July-August.

The bark on young trunks is reddish-brown, rather smooth, marked by large horizontally elongated light colored breathing pores (lenticels). The outer bark peels off readily in thin layers and exposes the green, very bitter inner bark. The twigs are slender, smooth, bright red, often covered with a thin gray coating which rubs off easily. They are marked with numerous pale to yellowish breathing pores, have a bitter taste and a peculiar odor.

The pin cherry acts as a nurse tree for other, more valuable trees and provides food for birds and other wildlife. The wood is light and soft with light brown heartwood and thin yellowish sapwood.

Pin Cherry

Range: The pin cherry is found from
Newfoundland to British Columbia, Georgia, and
Colorado. It is found throughout the northern
portion of the Great Lakes region and becomes rarer
south. This tree is common along fences and
roadsides, in abandoned fields, and rocky woods,
particularly on clearings and cut-over areas.

Mountain Ash

Pyrus americana

The mountain ash is one of our small forest trees, rarely exceeding 30 feet in height and 14 inches in diameter. It is essentially a tree of the north woods, being found commonly at high altitudes or in and about cool swamps.

The leaves are alternate, 6 to 10 inches long, compound, with 13 to 17 stalkless leaflets. The leaflets occur in pairs, except the terminal ones and are 2 to 3 inches long, sharp-pointed, finely toothed along the margin, and turn a bright yellow in autumn.

The fruit is a bright red, round berry, about the size of a pea, and arranged in flat-topped clusters 3 to 4 inches wide.

The bark is thin, smooth, grayish, somewhat scaly. The twigs are stout, smooth, grayish to reddish-brown, marked with pale dots and contain brownish pith. The buds are purplish-red, smooth or slightly hairy on the outside and densely hairy on the inside. The terminal buds are about ¼ of an inch long, conical, sharp-pointed, and covered with 2 or 3 visible scales.

The wood is soft, weak, close-grained, and brownish. It is not used commercially. A close relative, the European mountain ash (*Pyrus acuparia*) , is planted extensively as an ornamental.

Mountain Ash

Range: The mountain ash is found from
Newfoundland to Manitoba, southward to Iowa and
Pennsylvania and along the mountains to North
Carolina. It is found throughout the Great Lakes
region, especially in the northern portions.

Serviceberry

Amelanchier canadensis

The serviceberry, also called shad bush, june berry and service, is one of the most conspicuous small trees when in full bloom early in the spring. The early settlers observed that it was in full bloom when the shad ascended the rivers to spawn.

The leaves are simple, alternate, egg-shaped, 3 to 4 inches long, sharp-pointed, finely toothed along the margin and when young finely hairy and later smooth.

The flowers appear just when the leaves start to come out. They are white, stalked and arranged in drooping clusters 3 to 5 inches long.

The fruit is a reddish-purple sweet berry, about ⅓ of an inch in diameter, coated with whitish bloom when fully ripe, and matures in June or July.

The bark is usually smooth, grayish, often marked with black streaks. The twigs are slender, bright green to purplish-brown, smooth, and marked with scattered dots. The buds are slender, conical, ½ to ¾ of an inch long, 3 to 4 times as long as wide, sharp-pointed and greenish-brown.

The wood is heavy, hard, light to dark brown and checks and warps easily. It is rarely used for commercial purposes.

The tree rarely exceeds 25 feet in height and 12 inches in diameter. It is favored as an ornamental.

Serviceberry

Range: The service berry is found from
Newfoundland west to Kansas and south to Florida
and Louisiana. It is common throughout the region
and is often found in clumps along the border of
forests, along fences, roads, and water courses.

Hawthorn

Crataegus sp.

The hawthorns comprise a large group of small trees. Before 1900, not more than 75 different species were known. Now, more than 700 distinct species have been described by botanists.

If one observes the flowers and fruit of the hawthorns, it is easy to see that they are closely related to the apples, plums, and peaches. Two of the commonest and most distinctive hawthorns are the cockspur thorn and the dotted thorn.

The cockspur thorn (*Crataegus crusgalli*) may be recognized by its long, usually unbranched, chestnut brown thorns, its inversely ovate leaves, and its small, nearly spherical buds. The white flowers are grouped in round-topped clusters and the bright apple-like fruit persists far into winter.

The dotted thorn (*Crataegus punctata*) is one of the commonest thorns of the region although it is not found in great abundance in the northwest portion. Its leaves are simple, alternate, 2 to 3 inches long, wedge-shaped at the base, and irregularly toothed along the margin. When mature, the leaves are smooth with deeply impressed veins or the upper surface. The white flowers occur in clusters. The fruit is ½ to 1 inch long, dull red (sometimes yellow) with white dots. The branches and trunk are usually covered with rigid thorns.

Cockspur Thorn

Range: Hawthorns are found throughout the Great Lakes region and the U.S. as a small tree in mature hardwoods as well as in overgrown fields. Various species have been planted extensively as ornamentals.

PawPaw
Asimina triloba

The pawpaw is a dainty tree rarely exceeding 30 feet in height. A mere glance at the tree in summer suggests that it has escaped from the tropics for its leaves are truly tropical and its fruit resembles a stubby banana.

The leaves are simple, alternate, 4 to 12 inches long, thin in texture, short-pointed, long tapering at the base and smooth on the margin.

The flowers are large, 1 to 1½ inches wide, solitary, at first green, later reddish, occur below the leaves and are borne on short stalks.

The fruit is 3 to 5 inches long, at first green, yellowish to dark brown when ripe, and contains many dark brown, shiny, flat seeds throughout its edible flesh.

The bark is thin, smooth, dark brown, and often dotted. The twigs are rather slender, smooth, olive brown, and enlarged at nodes. The buds are brown, naked, and hairy. Terminal buds are large and flattened. Flower buds are round, 1/6 of an inch in diameter, very hairy and dark brown.

The wood is soft, weak, yellowish to brown. It is not used commercially.

The pawpaw is sometimes favored as an ornamental because of the unusual form of its leaves and fruit.

Pawpaw

Range: The pawpaw is found from western New York and New Jersey south to Florida and west to Michigan and Texas. It is found only in the extreme southern portion of the region.

Black Locust
Robinia pseudoacacia

The black locust, also called yellow locust and acacia, is a valuable and when in full bloom, a beautiful forest tree. It is unquestionably the best-known pod-bearing tree and it reaches a height of 50 to 75 feet and a diameter of 2 to 3 feet.

The leaves are alternate, compound, with 7 to 21 leaflets, 8 to 14 inches long. Leaflets are usually odd in number, short-stalked, 1 to 2 inches long.

The flowers appear in May or June and are cream-white, fragrant, resemble a pea blossom, and are arranged in drooping clusters 4 to 5 inches long. Some blossoms have pink stripes running longitudinally.

The fruit is a small, dark-brown, thin pod, 2 to 4 inches long, ½ of an inch wide, and contains 4 to 8 small brown seeds.

The bark on both young and old trunks is reddish-brown, and becomes thick and deeply furrowed. The twigs are stout, brittle, greenish to reddish-brown, and bear two short spines at each node. The buds are small, imbedded in the bark, and 3 to 4 occur above each other.

The wood is yellowish-brown, very heavy, hard and durable. The wood was once used to form wooden nails for early shipbuilding. It was introduced to Europe by the French king Louis IV.

Black Locust

Range: The black locust is found from the mountains of Pennsylvania south to Georgia, west to Iowa and Kansas. This tree is not native to the Great Lakes region but has escaped from ornamental plantings. It is a sun-loving tree that is often found in groves.

Honey Locust
Gleditsia triancanthos

The honey locust, also called sweet locust, thorn tree and three-thorned acacia, is the most beautiful pod-bearing tree found in the region.

The leaves are alternate, singly or doubly compound, 7 to 8 inches long. When singly compound, they have 18 to 28 leaflets, and when doubly compound have 8 to 14 pinnae each with 18 to 20 leaflets.

The flowers are greenish, appear about May or June, and are of two kinds. The pollen-bearing are arranged in short tassels; the pod-bearing occur in few-flowered clusters.

The fruit is a thin, flat, more or less twisted; reddish-brown pod, 10 to 18 inches long, containing many small flat seeds and often persist far into winter.

The bark on young stems is smooth, brownish, dotted with many oblong breathing pores. On old trunks it becomes grayish-brown to black and roughened with shallow furrows and firm ridges. The branches and trunk usually bear very distinctive, large, three-pronged sharp-pointed thorns. The twigs are smooth, glossy, and greenish-brown. The buds are very small, usually 3 at a node, and placed above one another.

The wood is hard, heavy, and strong.

Honey Locust

Region: The honey locust has a rather extensive range from Ontario to Kansas and south to Pennsylvania, Florida and Texas. Although this tree was native only in the southern portions of the Great Lakes region, a thornless variety has been planted extensively as an ornamental.

Kentucky Coffee Tree

Gymnocladus dioica

The Kentucky coffee tree, also called coffee nut and mahogany, attracts attention because of its unusual features. Its only close relative is native to China.

The leaves are alternate, twice and sometimes thrice compound, 10 to 3 feet long, 1½ to 2 feet wide. Leaflets are egg-shaped, about 2 inches long, sharp-pointed at the apex, and smooth to wavy along the margin.

The flowers appear about June and are of two kinds. The pollen-bearing are greenish-white, arranged in clusters 3 to 4 inches long. The pod-producing are greenish-white and grouped in clusters 6 to 8 inches long. The fruit is a broad, flat, thick, stubby, reddish-brown pod, 4 to 10 inches long, 2 to 4 inches broad. Pods contain 6 to 9 marble-like brown seeds and often persist far into winter.

The bark is dark gray to black-brown, roughened by long shallow furrows. The twigs are very stout, greenish-brown, often covered with a crusty coating, marked with large, broadly heart-shaped leaf scars and contain wide pinkish to brown pith. The buds are small, downy, almost entirely imbedded in twigs, surrounded by a hairy ring of bark, often placed above one another in close formations.

Kentucky Coffee Tree

Range: The Kentucky coffee tree is found from central New York to Tennessee, west to Minnesota and Oklahoma. It is most common in the southern portion of the Great Lakes region. It makes rich bottomlands its home where it reaches a height of 100 feet and a diameter of 3 feet.

Redbud

Cercis canadensis

The redbud, also called Judas tree, is one of the most attractive small trees native to the Great Lakes region. No tree has more striking distinguishing characteristics.

The leaves are simple, alternate, heart-shaped, 3 to 5 inches long, pointed at the apex and entire on the margin.

The flowers appear before the leaves and resemble sweet peas. They are brilliant red and occur in numerous clusters of 4 to 8 along twigs.

The fruit is a small rose-colored to light-brown, short-stalked, thin flat pod, 2½ to 3 inches long, about ½ an inch wide, and contains 4 to 8 light-brown flat seeds.

The bark is thin, reddish-brown, and peels off into thin scales. The twigs are slender, smooth, light brown, buds are small, spherical, ⅛ of an inch across, dark purplish-red, and usually occur one above another and often are grouped in small clusters at the base of lateral branches.

The wood is heavy, hard, dark reddish-brown with light sapwood. It is of no commercial importance.

The redbud is a very popular ornamental tree and is used extensively throughout the Great Lakes region.

Redbud

Range: The redbud is found from Ontario to Minnesota, south to Florida and Arkansas. It is primarily found in rich fertile lowlands and moist hillsides in the southern portion of the Great Lake region.

Ailanthus

Ailanthus altissima

The ailanthus, also called tree of heaven, is an interesting tree immigrant that came to this country from China about 200 years ago and was first planted near Philadelphia.

The leaves are alternate, compound, with 11 to 31 leaflets, usually 1 to 2 feet, but occasionally 3 feet long. Leaflets are 3 to 5 inches long, egg-shaped, long-pointed at the apex, and smooth along the margin except for a few teeth near the base. They produce unpleasant smells when crushed. Glands are usually present near the base of leaflets.

The flowers are small, greenish, of two kinds and arranged in loose clusters. Pollen-bearing and seed-producing occur on different trees. The fruit is a thin winged seed produced in large clusters. The bark on young trees is smooth, thin, light gray. On older trunks it becomes dark gray to black and shallowly furrowed. The twigs are very stout, yellowish-green to brown, covered with a velvety down, and marked with ochre-colored breathing pores and large heart-shaped leaf scars with 8 to 14 groups of bundle scars. The buds are small, round and reddish-brown.

The wood is light, soft, weak, white to pale yellow. The wood can be used for paper pulp.

This is a hardy tree and adapts well to the city.

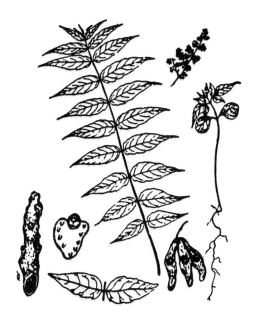

Ailanthus

Range: The ailanthus is not native to the region but has been planted rather widely in the southern portions. Its odd appearance, heavy foliage, rapid growth and ability to grown in a variety of soils make it a good choice for urban waste areas.

Horse Chestnut

Aesculus hippocastaneum

The horse chestnut has been carried by man from its original home in the mountains of Greece over a considerable part of the civilized world.

The leaves are opposite, compound, with 5 to 7 leaflets, obversely egg-shaped, arranged in a fan-like form. The flowers appear in May or June, are large, white, with throats dotted with yellow and purple and arranged in upright clusters 8 to 12 inches high. The fruit is a leathery round capsule about 2 inches across, roughened with spines and contain 1 to 3 shiny brown nuts.

The bark is dark brown, breaks up into thin plates which peel off slowly. The twigs are stout, reddish-brown, smooth, obscurely dotted with breathing pores and marked with large horseshoe-like scars, each with 5 to 7 groups of bundle scars. The buds are large, sticky, varnished, reddish-brown.

The wood is light, soft, weak, whitish. The horse chestnut is a sturdy, rapid-growing tree. It is found along some streets having been planted as an ornamental. A similar tree, the Ohio buckeye, is a native of the Mississippi Valley and is also planted as an ornamental in the Great Lakes region.

Note that there is little similarity between the horse chestnut and the American Chestnut.

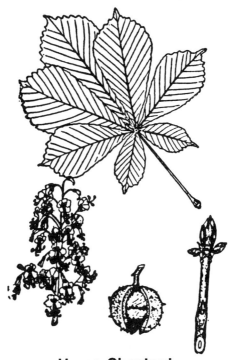

Horse Chestnut

Range: The horse chestnut has been planted widely as an ornamental and is now found in every state in the U.S. It is not native to the U.S. but has spread rapidly on its own.

Staghorn Sumac

Rhus typhina

The staghorn sumac, also called velvet sumac, is the largest of the native sumacs. Under favorable conditions, it reaches a height of 35 feet and a diameter of 8 inches.

The leaves are alternate, 16 to 24 inches long, compound, with 11 to 31 leaflets. Leaf stalks are hairy. Leaf scars are U-shaped and contain 3 groups of small greenish bundle scars.

The flowers are small, greenish yellow, appear about May, occur in Pyramid-like panicles 5 to 12 inches long and 4 to 6 inches broad.

The fruit is a small red drupe arranged in erect, red heads 5 to 8 inches long and 4 to 6 inches broad.

The bark on old trunks is rough, dark brown; on younger trunks it is smooth, thin, and covered with numerous yellowish-brown dots. The twigs are stout, covered with a dense coating of velvety hairs, contain a wide yellowish-brown pith, and when cut or bruised they yield a milky sap. The buds are small, round and hairy.

The wood is soft, brittle, rather satiny to touch, orange colored streaked with green. It is common on abandoned fields and fence rows. The staghorn sumac is prized for its color.

Staghorn Sumac

Range: The staghorn sumac is found from New Brunswick to Minnesota, south to Georgia. This large shrub or small tree is found in southern Michigan. Fertile, dry uplands are its favorite home.

Poison Sumac

Rhus vernix

The poison sumac, also called poison elder and swamp sumac, differs from the other sumac in that it produces ivory-white tree fruit.

The leaves are alternate, 7 to 14 inches long, compound with 7 to 13 leaflets. The leaflets are 3 to 4 inches long, narrowly egg-shaped, smooth along the margin, and dark green and shiny above and paler on the lower surface.

The flowers appear in June or July. The pollen-bearing and seed-producing occur on different trees. They are small, yellowish-green, arranged in drooping panicles. The fruit is a small, round, glossy, ivory-white drupe, arranged in lose drooping clusters.

The bark is smooth, somewhat streaked, light to dark gray, and marked with elongated dots. The twigs are stout, orange-brown, smooth, and glossy. The buds are purplish, about 2/5 of an inch long, and sharp-pointed.

The wood is soft, brittle, coarse-grained, and light yellow.

This tree carries the same skin toxins as poison ivy and can cause very painful welts that also itch. Like poison ivy, it should be recognized and avoided. Washing thoroughly immediately after exposure will reduce or eliminate the welts.

Poison Sumac

Range: The poison sumac is found from Ontario to
Minnesota south to Florida and Louisiana. It is
primarily found in swamps and bogs in the southern
portion of the region.

Sugar Maple

Acer saccharum

The sugar maple, also called hard maple and rock maple, is probably the best-known American hardwood tree.

The leaves are simple, opposite, 3 to 5 inches long, coarsely toothed, dark green above and pale below.

The flowers are yellowish-green and appear in April and May with the leaves. Both pollen-bearing and seed-producing flowers occur in drooping, slender-stalked clusters on the new growth.

The fruit is a two-winged maple key. The wings are about an inch long and are almost parallel to each other or slightly divergent.

The bark is grayish to brownish black, roughened with shallow furrows. The twigs are slender, smooth, reddish to orange brown, and marked with pale dots. The buds are brown, conical, sharp-pointed, and covered with 8 to 10 expose scales.

The wood is heavy, hard, close-grained, light brown to reddish. It is an all-purpose wood as it is used for a wide variety of wood products, including fuel.

It is from this tree that the sweet sap is gathered in the spring and evaporated to obtain maple sugar and syrup.

Sugar Maple

Range: The sugar maple is found from Newfoundland to Manitoba, south to Florida and Texas. It occurs in every state east of the Mississippi River but is rare in the south. It is found throughout the Great Lakes region. It can reach a height of 100 feet and a diameter of 4 feet.

Black Maple

Acer nigrum

The black maple, also called black sugar, is one of the most interesting and attractive trees of the region.

The leaves are simple, opposite, 3 to 6 inches long, often wider than long, with 3 main lobes and 2 smaller lower lobes. The leaves are yellow-green beneath and rich green above. The lower lobes of the leaves have a tendency to droop. The base of the leaf stalks of the terminal leaves are enlarged at the base and smooth or somewhat hairy about the enlarged base. By maturity, a scale-like appendage often develops on each side of the base of the leaf stalks.

The flowers, fruit, twigs, buds, and wood are similar to those of the sugar maple. The bark is darker and narrower and shallower than that of the sugar maple. Like the sugar maple, the black maple is tapped in the spring for its sweet sap that is evaporated into syrup and sugar.

The black maple prefers low, moist situations and rich river bottoms but it also does well on gravelly upland soils. It is a medium to larger tree which produces good wood, lives long, holds its foliage long, is relatively free from insect and fungus attack, and develops an attractive form. It is a tree prized for shade and ornamental planting.

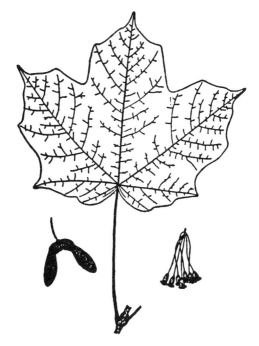

Black Maple

Range: The black maple is found from Quebec west to South Dakota and south to Georgia and Louisiana. This tree is especially common in the southeastern portions of the Great Lakes region.

Silver Maple

Acer saccharinum

The silver maple, also called white maple, soft maple and river maple, is one of the best-known American trees on account of its wide natural range and its general use for shade and ornamental planting.

The leaves are simple, opposite, 5-lobed, silvery white on the lower surfaces and divided by deep clefts with rounded bases. The base of the clefts of the red maple are sharp-angled.

The flowers are reddish to crimson and occur in compact clusters along twigs early in the spring before the leaves appear.

The fruit is a typical two-winged maple key. The wings are 2 to 3 inches long and wide spreading.

The bark on branches and young stems is smooth and gray; on old trunks it becomes grayish brown and separates into thin flakes. The twigs are slender, glossy, reddish-brown and have a disagreeable odor if broken. They are marked with many light dots. The buds are round, red, covered with 6 to 8 visible scales and clustered in groups along twigs.

The wood is hard, rather brittle, close-grained and light brown with wide, white sapwood. It is used for paper pulp. The tree grows rapidly and reaches a height of 80 feet and a diameter of 3 feet.

Silver Maple

Range: The silver maple is found from New Brunswick to Florida and west to the Dakotas and Oklahoma. In the Great Lakes region it is found primarily in the southern portions. It prefers moist situations and is found along streams and ponds.

Red Maple

Acer rubrum

At all seasons of the year, the red maple, also called scarlet maple, soft maple, swamp maple and water maple, is a beautiful red. In autumn it is at its best. Then, it stands out among its associates as a flaming torch of scarlet and crimson.

The leaves are simple, opposite, about 3 inches long, 3 to 5 lobed, pale green to whitish on lower surfaces. The clefts between lobes are shallow and sharp-angled.

The flowers are red and appear early in the spring before the leaves and are arranged in numerous small clusters.

The fruit is a typical two-winged maple key. The wings are less than an inch long and not wide spreading from each other.

The bark on branches and young trunks is smooth and gray; on older trunks it is grayish brown and shags off in small thin plates. The twigs are smooth, red, and marked with light dots. The buds are round, red, and covered with 6 to 8 exposed scales. They are clustered in groups along twigs. They are similar to those of the silver maple.

The red maple has rare beauty, produces good wood and grows to a height of 100 feet and a diameter of 4 feet. It is usually 40 to 60 feet high. It blossoms early when bees visit in large numbers.

Red Maple

Range: The red maple is one of the most widely distributed trees of North America. This tree is found throughout the Great Lakes region in wet to swampy situations, fertile lowlands, and moist hillsides.

Box Elder

Acer negundo

The box elder, also called ash-leaved maple and water ash, is the only maple of the region with compound leaves. All other maples have simple leaves. It is a sturdy tree, usually 30 to 50 feet high.

The leaves are opposite, compound, with 3 to 5 leaflets. Leaflets are 2 to 4 inches long and coarsely toothed. The leaf scars complete encircle the twigs.

The flowers are yellowish-green suspended on slender stalks in small open clusters. The pollen-bearing and the seed producing occur on different trees.

The fruit is a typical two-winged maple key, which matures about September. They occur in drooping clusters, often persisting far into winter. The wings are 1½ to 2 inches long and usually incurved.

The bark on branches and young trunks is smooth and grayish-brown; on older trunks it becomes dark and breaks up into shallow furrows. The twigs are stout, greenish to purplish green, smooth, and often covered with a whitish crusty coating. The buds are rather large, egg-shaped, short-stalked, white-woolly, and grouped at nodes in clusters of 2 to 3. The outer pair of bud scales completely covers the inner pair.

The wood is light and soft and not durable.

Box Elder

Range: The box elder is widely distributed from New England to Alberta, south to Florida, Texas and Mexico. It is most common locally in the southern portions of the region. It prefers moist situations and grows rapidly.

Striped Maple

Acer pennsylvanicum

The striped maple, also called moosewood and whistlewood, is one of the most attractive and distinctive trees in the forests of the Great Lakes region.

The leaves are simple, opposite, goose foot-like, 3-lobed with rusty brown to reddish hairs on the lower surface.

The flowers are small, bell-shaped, greenish to yellow and arranged in drooping clusters 3 to 4 inches long.

The fruit is a two-winged maple key. The wings are about ¾ of an inch long and rather divergent.

The twigs are stout, smooth, reddish, marked with a few dots, and contain brown pith. The buds are 2/5 of an inch long, obviously stalked and covered with two visible red scales.

The wood is light, soft and of no commercial importance although it is used in the manufacture of paper.

This tree rarely exceeds 30 feet in height and is widely planted as an ornamental because of its rare beauty. Deer and moose browse freely on the green shoots.

The striped maple prefers moist, cool, and shaded slopes and ravines.

Striped Maple

Range: The striped maple is found from Nova Scotia to Minnesota and south to Pennsylvania and along the mountains to Georgia. It is abundant in the northern portions of the Great Lakes region.

Mountain Maple

Acer spicatum

The mountain maple has a good name for it is truly a tree of the mountains. One usually finds it grown on rocky hillsides and along the border of ravines. It seldom exceeds 25 feet in height.

The leaves are simple, opposite, usually 3-lobed, 3 to 5 inches long, coarsely toothed and light and hairy on the lower surface.

The flowers do not appear until early summer. They are white and arranged in erect spikes about 3 inches long.

The fruit is a typical maple key ripening in autumn and often hanging into winter. The fruit keys are the smallest of the native maples.

A close examination of the reddish-brown twigs shows them covered with a whitish coating of fine hairs. The buds are ¼ of an inch long, blunt-pointed, short-stalked, and covered with a few visible greenish to grayish scales.

The mountain maple is common in the understory of the forest. Although used for paper manufacturing, it is of no great economic importance. It is, however, desirable for ornamental planting and to prevent erosion. Also, deer browse on the tender twigs and shoots of this tree.

Mountain Maple

Range: The mountain maple is found from
Newfoundland to Manitoba, south to Michigan and
Pennsylvania and along the mountains to Georgia.
This tree is common in the northern portions of the
Great Lakes region.

Norway Maple

Acer platanoides

The Norway maple is one of the most popular street trees in the United States. There are very few cities in which this tree is not found. It comes to us from Europe where it is found from Norway to Switzerland.

The leaves resemble those of the sugar maple but are deeper green in color and firmer in texture. One characteristic by which it can always be distinguished is the presence of milky sap in the leaf stalks. If pressed or twisted, the leaf stalks always yield a few drops of milky sap.

In early spring the yellowish-green flowers arranged in clusters along the twigs are distinctive. In winter, the large, red, blunt-pointed glossy buds are a sure means of identification. In late summer, the large fruit keys with wide-spreading wings ripen and may hang on the tree for months.

The Norway maple is rather free from disease and insect attacks. It retains its leaves longer than the native maples and endures the smoke and dust of the city. These characteristics have made it a popular tree for shade and ornamental plantings.

Another European maple planted in the region is the sycamore maple (*Acer pseudoplatanus*). It can be distinguished by its 3 to 5-lobed leaves, sharply toothed margins and blunt-pointed green buds.

Norway Maple

Range: The norway maple is widely distributed in the Great Lakes region. Because it was introduced from Europe as a shade and ornamental tree, it is most often found in city parks and along streets.

Basswood

Tilia americana

The basswood is a tree of many names. Among them are linden, lynn, lime-tree, whitewood, beetree and whistlewood.

The leaves are simple, alternate, egg-shaped to round, 4 to 7 inches long, firm in texture, toothed along the margins, and unequally heart-shaped at the base. Tufts of rusty hair often occur in axils of the veins.

The flowers appear in June or July. They are small, yellowish-white, sweet, fragrant, 5 to 20 in a cluster, and attached to a wing-like bract by a slender stalk.

The fruit is a wood nut-like berry about the size of a pea. It usually occurs in small clusters attached to a wing-like bract by slender stalks and often persists far into winter.

The bark on young stems is smooth and dark gray. On older trunks it becomes thick and clearly furrowed. The twigs are smooth, shiny, rather stout and bright red. The buds are egg-shaped, 2-ranked, stout, blunt-pointed, usually deep red, and have 3 visible bud scales.

The wood is light, soft, light brown to nearly white. It is used in the manufacture of paper and some household items. It reaches a height of 70 to 80 feet and spouts freely.

Basswood

Range: The basswood is found from New
Brunswick to Manitoba, southward to Georgia and
Texas. The tree is abundant throughout much of the
Great Lakes region, particularly in the northern
portions. It prefers rich, moist bottomlands and
hillsides.

Flowering Dogwood

Cornus florida

The flowering dogwood is among the best-known small trees of eastern North America. Early in the spring it bursts forth in floral beauty and in autumn it is an attractive member of the understory of the forest.

The leaves are simple, opposite, 3 to 5 inches long, 2 to 3 inches wide, smooth or wavy along the margins, and often clustered at the end of twigs. In autumn the leaves become a beautiful red.

The flowers appear about April in greenish clusters surrounded by large white bracts.

The fruit is a scarlet berry about 3/5 of an inch long, arranged in clusters of 2 to 5.

The bark on young stems is smooth, light brown to reddish-gray; on old stems it becomes reddish-brown and divides into squarish blocks.

The twigs are usually smooth, red, tinged with green and often glossy. The flower buds are goblet-like, about 2/5 of an inch in diameter. The leaf buds are smaller, flattened, and slightly hairy.

The wood is hard, heavy, strong, reddish-brown to pinkish with light sapwood. It is used for tool handles and household items.

This tree is usually found as an understory plant of the forest. It rarely exceeds 30 feet in height and 8 inches in diameter.

Flowering Dogwood

Range: The flowering dogwood is found from
Massachusetts to Michigan, Florida, and Texas. It is
found primarily in the southern portions of the
region.

Black Gum

Nyssa sylvatica

The black gum, also called sour gum, tupelo, and pepperidge, is at its best in autumn when the entire crown is often clothed with a complete garment of flaming red.

In winter, when the foliage is off, it has a strikingly picturesque form. The stem often continues from the base to the tip without dividing. In young and middle-aged trees, the top branches take an upright position, the lower ones droop while those along the middle stand out horizontally.

The leaves are simple, alternate, 2 to 5 inches long, oval, blunt-pointed, wedge-shaped at the base and smooth along the margin.

The twigs are smooth, grayish-brown, and dotted with crescent-shaped leaf scars each marked with three distinct bundle scars. The buds are reddish-brown and scattered alternately along the twigs.

On young trunks the bark is smooth to scaly. It breaks into squarish reddish-brown to black blocks on older stems.

The fruit is a dark blue fleshy berry about ⅔ of an inch long. Each berry contains a single hard-shelled seed. Several berries usually occur in a slender-stalked cluster. Some birds eat the berries.

The black gun rarely exceeds 60 feet in height and 2 feet in diameter.

Black Gum

Range: The black gum is found from Maine to Florida, west to Michigan and Texas. It is common in the southern portions of the Great Lakes region and favors wet situations.

White Ash

Fraxinus americana

The white ash is the most beautiful and useful of our native ashes. It stand among the most important forest trees.

The leaves are opposite, about 10 inches long and compound with 5 to 9 leaflets. Leaflets are 3 to 5 inches long, evidently stalked, smooth or obscurely toothed on the margin, smooth and dark green above and silvery white below.

The flowers are of two kinds. The pollen-bearing occur in dense reddish-purple clusters, the seed-producing in rather open panicles.

The fruit is a winged seed, 1 to 2 inches long. The wing is long, narrow and attached to the end of the seed. The seeds are grouped in loose drooping clusters.

The grayish-brown, and rather thick bark soon becomes rough, dividing into diamond-shaped fissures. The twigs are smooth, grayish-brown and flattened at nodes. They are marked with scattered pale dots. Terminal buds are larger that lateral buds.

The wood is very heavy, hard, tough, elastic, with light sapwood and brownish heartwood. It is used widely particularly for athletic equipment, tools, furniture, and interior finishings.

This tree becomes large--often 70 to 80 feet high and 3 feet in diameter--and grows rapidly.

White Ash

Range: The white ash is found from Nova Scotia to Minnesota to Florida and Texas. It is common throughout the Great Lakes region and prefers moist woods and borders of lakes and streams.

Black Ash

Fraxinus nigra

The black ash is a tree of the swamps or other moist places. The early settlers called it hoop ash and the American Indians called it basket ash for the products that could be manufactured from its wood.

The leaves are opposite, 10 to 14 inches long, compound, with 7 to 11 leaflets. The leaflets are 3 to 5 inches long, finely toothed along the margin, and all are stalkless except the terminal leaflet.

The flowers are similar to those of the white ash.

The fruit is a winged seed similar to that of the white ash but is broader winged, notched at the apex, and the wing completely surrounds the flattened seed.

The bark is thin, grayish, very shallowly furrowed, and peels off in powdery to corky fine scales. The twigs are smooth, stout, light-gray. The buds are opposite, black, and sharp-pointed.

The wood is soft, rather coarse-grained, with white sapwood and dark brown heartwood. It is used for many household items and interior finishings. The wood is rather ordinary and the tree is rarely used as an ornamental.

The black ash usually has a slender stem and may reach a height of 60 to 80 feet.

Black Ash

Range: The black ash is found from Newfoundland
to Manitoba, south to Virginia and Arkansas. It is
found throughout the Great Lakes region where it
prefers moist situations, such as swamps and low
river flats, although it may grow on upland soils.

Blue Ash

Fraxinus quadrangulata

The blue ash is perhaps the easiest of all our native ash trees to recognize.

At all seasons of the year it can be identified by its four-sided twigs with four ridges projecting out from the bark. The four ridges are frequently a lighter brown than the twigs themselves.

On very vigorous shoots, corky bark yields a blue coloring if mixed with water, hence its name, blue ash.

The leaves are opposite, greenish-yellow, compound, with 7 to 11 leaflets borne on very short stalks or sometimes stalkless. The veins, midribs, and leaflet stalks are permanently pubescent. The rest of the leaf is generally smooth.

The fruit is winged to the base. The wing completely surrounds the seed. It resembles that of the black ash.

The bark is light gray, scaly or flaky, not fissured. It is similar to that of the black ash.

The wood is intermediate in quality between that of white ash and black ash and is generally sold as white ash.

The blue ash is not common anywhere in the Great Lakes region and is usually seen solitary on rich limestone hills and also on fertile bottomlands.

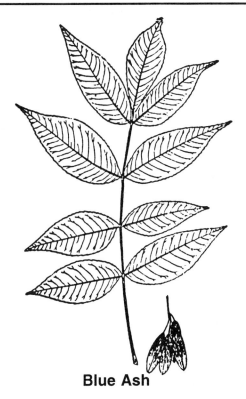

Blue Ash

Range: The blue ash ranges from southern Ontario to Iowa and south to northern Alabama and Arkansas. In the Great Lakes region this tree is generally found in the southern portions.

Catalpa
Catalpa speciosa

The hardy catalpa, also called catalfa, Indian bean, and cigar tree, was formerly planted widely on account of its reputed rapid growth, and its very durable wood.

The leaves are simple, opposite or 3 may occur in a whorl. They are heart-shaped at the base, long taper-pointed, 6 to 10 inches long and 4 to 5 inches wide. The odor of the bruised leaves is putrid.

The flowers appear in May or June. They are white with yellowish and purplish spots within and arranged in large, erect clusters 8 to 10 inches high. The lower lobe of the corolla is notched.

The fruit is a long bean-like capsule containing many flat-winged seeds. It often persists far into winter.

The bark on old trees is fissured and ridgy and dark grayish-brown. The twigs are stout, smooth, yellowish-brown and marked with large leaf scars. The buds are very small, less that ⅛ of an inch long and often imbedded in the bark.

The wood is durable, light brown, with a satiny surface and kerosene-like odor. It is especially well-suited for fence posts and rails.

The catalpa has been planted extensively in the region as an ornamental tree. Thrifty trees develop straight trunks and reach a large size in the forest.

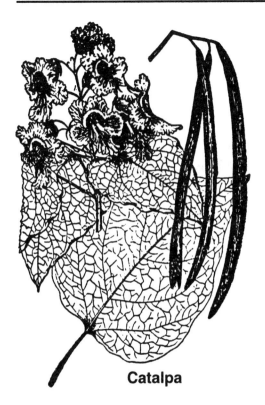

Catalpa

Range: The catalpa was originally native from southwestern Indiana to southeastern Missouri and northeastern Arkansas. It has been planted in the Great Lakes region as an ornamental and shade tree.

Poison Ivy
Toxicodendron radicans

Poison ivy can be identified by its three notched leaflets. The plant may be found growing close to the ground in dense forests or near open beaches.

Contact with poison ivy transfers a potent toxin to the skin or clothes. This substance frequently causes itching and blisters. Washing the skin and clothes can help avoid discomfort. It is best to recognize the plant and avoid it.

Key to Common Trees

I. **Trees with needle-like or scale-like leaves; fruit a cone or cone-like (conifers).**
   A. Leaves needle-like.
      1. Leaves in bundles or on clusters
         a) Leaves in bundles
            1. Leaves or needles in 5's ....**white pine**
            2. Leaves or needles in 2's
               a. leaves 4-6".....................................**red pine**
               b. leaves 1-2"....................................**jack pine**
         b) Leaves in clusters, soft and flexible, shed in fall..**tamarack**
      2. Leaves not in bundles
         a) Leaves flattened.
            1. Leaves ½ inch long, cones ½ to ¾ inch and pendent...**hemlock**
            2. Leaves ¾ inch long, cones 2 to 3 inches and erect..**balsam fir**
         b) Leaves four sided.
            1. Branchlets smooth, needles ill-scented, 1 to 2 inch cones...................................**white spruce**
            2. Branchlets hairy, short needles, pleasantly scented, ½ to ¾ inch cones........**black spruce**
   B. Leaves scale-like
      1. Branchlets flattened in fan-like sprays, fruit reddish brown..**white cedar**
      2. Branchlets 4 angled, not in fan-like sprays, fruit berry-like and dark blue............................**red cedar**

II. Trees with broad, flat leaves of many shapes and patterns (broad leaf trees).

A. Leaves compound.
  1. Opposite.
    a) Palmately compound; seven leaflets
    ....**horse chestnut**
    b) Pinnately compound.
      1. Leaf margins entire or finely toothed, leaflets distinctly petioled; fruit a single samara...**ashes**
      2. Leaf margins coarsely toothed or lobed, leaflets somewhat petioled or sessile; fruit a double samara..................................**box elder**
  2. Alternate.
    a) Leaflets small, less than 2 inches long; fruit a pod, branches with thorns...............**honey locust**
    b) Leaflets large, more than 2 inches long.
      1. Fruit, a pod, 4 to 10 inches long, reddish brown.............................**Kentucky coffee tree**
      2. Fruit a drupe, 3/16 inches on an erect conical cluster......................**staghorn sumac**
      3. Fruit a nut; twig pith chambered.
        a. Pith, buff colored....................**black walnut**
        b. Pith, chocolate colored................**butternut**
      4. Fruit a nut; twig-pith homogeneous
      ....**true hickories**

B. Leaves simple.
  1. Leaves opposite.
    a) Leaves lobed (star-like); fruit a samara....**maples**
    b) leaves not lobed
      1. Large, heart-shaped; fruit a cylindrical pod 6 to 14 inches long.................................**catalpa**
      2. Small to medium, ovate; fruit a red berry, borne in clusters................**flowering dogwood**

2. Leaves alternate.
   a) Leaves lobed or notched
      1. Leaves as wide as they are long.
         a. Twigs and leaves aromatic, leaves of three forms; entire, mitten-shaped and 3-lobed..**sassafras**
         b. Twigs and leaves not aromatic, leaves of one form.
            i. Leaf margin entire, four-lobed; flower tulip-shaped.......................**yellow poplar**
            ii. Leaf margins not entire.
               (a) Leaf margin finely to coarsely toothed, petioles laterally flattened.............**cottonwood, aspen**
               (b) Leaf mitten-shaped, twigs zig-zag, fruit edible...........................**mulberry**
               (c) Leaf one form, pointed lobes, hollow petiole at base; old bark peels in thin curled pieces ....**sycamore**
      2. Leaves longer than wide.
         a. Leaves medium to large, fruit an acorn.
            i. Leaves bristle-tipped, inside of acorn shell hairy; kernel bitter ....**red or black oaks**
            ii. Leaves rounded; inside of acorn shell smooth; kernel sweet............**white oaks**
   b) Leaves not lobed or notched
      1. Leaves with unequal bases, one-sided as to midrib position
         a. Margins doubly serrated....................**elms**
         b. Margin not double serrated
            i. Leaf heart-shaped; fruit a small woody nut subtended by a leaf-like blade ....**basswood**

      ii. Leaf ovate; fruit a small dark red drupe,
         corky bark................................**hackberry**
  2. Leaves with an equal base (not one-sided)
    a. Leaf margin entire
      i. Spiny, toothed or bristle-like at the end
        of each vein; fruit a nut.
        (a) Bark smooth, blue-gray; terminal
           bud long, pointed; fruit a small
           triangular nut...........................**beech**
      ii. Margin finely or doubly serrated
        (a) Margin finely serrated
          (i) Fruit fleshy, leaves finely
             toothed, fruit a one-seeded
             drupe................................**cherry**
          (ii) Fruit not fleshy, leaf petiole
             short, leaves lance-shaped with
             long tapered tips...............**willow**
        (b) Margin double serrated
          (i) Bark white and peeling
        ....**white birch**
          (ii) Bark white and tight to tree
        ....**gray birch**
          (iii) Bark yellow and peeling,
             wintergreen taste....**yellow birch**

Shapes of Leaves

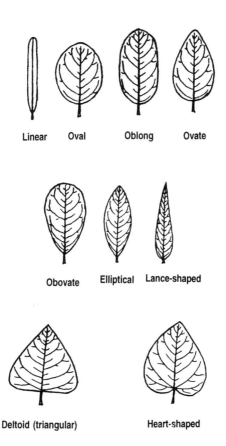

Linear   Oval   Oblong   Ovate

Obovate   Elliptical   Lance-shaped

Deltoid (triangular)   Heart-shaped

Types of Leaf Margins

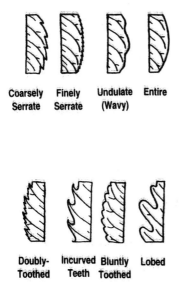

Coarsely Serrate   Finely Serrate   Undulate (Wavy)   Entire

Doubly-Toothed   Incurved Teeth   Bluntly Toothed   Lobed

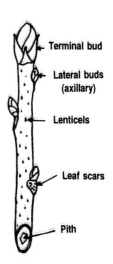

Terminal bud

Lateral buds (axillary)

Lenticels

Leaf scars

Pith

Twig with a Terminal Bud (Hickory)

182

Types of Buds

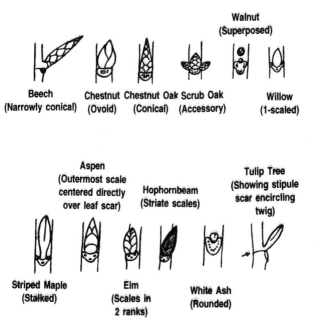

Walnut
(Superposed)

Beech
(Narrowly conical)

Chestnut
(Ovoid)

Chestnut Oak
(Conical)

Scrub Oak
(Accessory)

Willow
(1-scaled)

Aspen
(Outermost scale
centered directly
over leaf scar)

Hophornbeam
(Striate scales)

Tulip Tree
(Showing stipule
scar encircling
twig)

Striped Maple
(Stalked)

Elm
(Scales in
2 ranks)

White Ash
(Rounded)

Types of Fruits

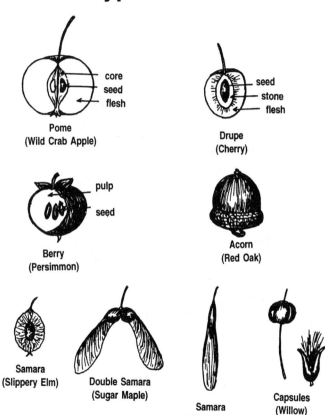

Pome
(Wild Crab Apple)

core
seed
flesh

Drupe
(Cherry)

seed
stone
flesh

Berry
(Persimmon)

pulp
seed

Acorn
(Red Oak)

Samara
(Slippery Elm)

Double Samara
(Sugar Maple)

Samara
(White Ash)

Capsules
(Willow)

Aggregate of
Follicles
(Magnolia)

Legume
(Black Locust)

Nut with Dehiscent Husk
(Shagbark Hickory)

Nutlet
(Hornbeam)

Cone
(Hemlock)

Aggregate of
Samaras
(Tulip Tree)

Strobile
Winged Nutlet
(Birch)

Multiple Fruit of
Small Drupes
(Red Mulberry)

Parts, Types and Positions of Leaves

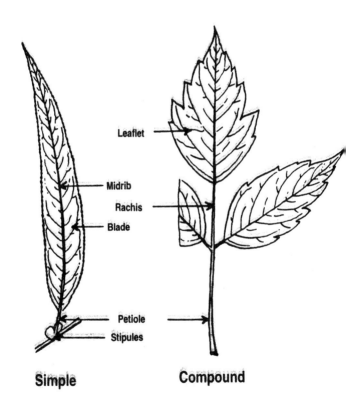

Leaflet

Midrib

Rachis

Blade

Petiole

Stipules

Simple

Compound

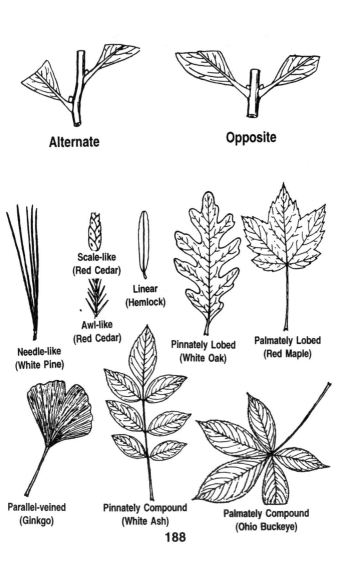

Alternate

Opposite

Scale-like
(Red Cedar)

Linear
(Hemlock)

Awl-like
(Red Cedar)

Needle-like
(White Pine)

Pinnately Lobed
(White Oak)

Palmately Lobed
(Red Maple)

Parallel-veined
(Ginkgo)

Pinnately Compound
(White Ash)

Palmately Compound
(Ohio Buckeye)

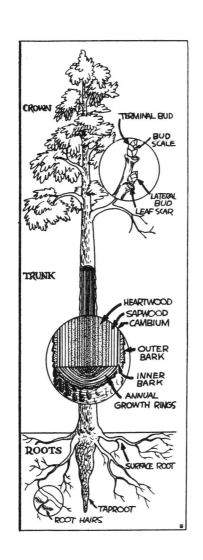

CROWN

TERMINAL BUD

BUD SCALE

LATERAL BUD

LEAF SCAR

TRUNK

HEARTWOOD

SAPWOOD

CAMBIUM

OUTER BARK

INNER BARK

ANNUAL GROWTH RINGS

ROOTS

SURFACE ROOT

TAPROOT

ROOT HAIRS

Definitions

bract--a small, leaf-like appendage at the base of a flower or flower cluster.

bud scale--modified leaves covering a bud.

catkin--a flexible, usually drooping stem bearing either male (pollen-producing) or female (fruit producing) flowers.

compound leaf--a leaf made up of several separate leaflets attached to a common leaf stem.

cone--a fruit with woody, overlapping scales.

conifer--a tree which produces its seeds in cones.

coniferous--a term applied to that group of trees which produces its seeds in cones.

deciduous--a term applied to those trees which lose their leaves annually, usually at the end of the growing season.

entire--a leaf with a smooth margin.

genus--a subdivision of a family composed of a closely related species, such as the oaks, genus *Quercus*.

glabrous--smooth, without hairs.

hardwood--in general the broad-leaved trees are classed as hardwoods. The term also applies to the lumber produced from these trees even though it may be fairly soft.

heartwood--the central core of a woody stem or trunk which gives it strength. It is composed of dead cells, and is often distinguished from the sapwood by its darker color.

leaf scar--the scar left on the twig where a leaf was attached. Leaf scars vary in size and shape with different species and are frequently useful in winter identification of hardwoods.

leaflet--one of the several separate division of a compound leaf.

lenticel--a corky growth on young or sometimes older bark, which admit air to the interior of the twig or branch.

mid rib--the central vein or main rib of a leaf.

mucilaginous--a plant structure that produces mucous.

node--the point of attachment of a leaf on a twig.

opposite--one plant structure found directly across from another, not alternate. For example, MAD Horse refers to the trees with opposite leaves, maples, ash, dogwood and horse chestnut.

panicle--a floral arrangement consisting of a central stalk supporting several flowers on short, branched stalks.

petiole--the stalk of a leaf.

pith--the interior (heartwood) found in the center of a twig.

pulpwood--wood cut primarily for the manufacture of paper and various pressed board products.

samara--a dry, single-seeded winged fruit.

sapwood--the living, usually light-colored, band of wood surrounding the heartwood, through which sap flows from the roots to the leaves.

serrate--toothed with fine, sharp teeth.

silviculture--the art of producing and tending a forest.

simple--a single leaf, not compound.

softwood--in general the coniferous trees are classed as softwoods. The term also applies to lumber produced from these trees.

species--generally the final subdivision in plant or animal classification, composed of individuals exhibiting identical biological characteristics.

spike--a floral arrangement consisting of a central stalk supporting several stemless flowers.

veneer--a thin sheet of wood peeled, sliced, or sawed from a log, generally a hardwood.

whorl--a spoke-like arrangement of leaves or branches around a stem.